Successor journal to *Theatre Quarterly* (1971–1981)
VOLUME XIII   NUMBER 52   NOVEMBER 1997

Editors
CLIVE BARKER
SIMON TRUSSLER

Contents

New Theatre Quarterly is published in February, May, August, and November by Cambridge University Press, The Edinburgh Building, Shaftesbury Road, Cambridge CB2 2RU, United Kingdom   ISBN 0 521 59729 3   ISSN 0266 – 464X

Editorial Enquiries
Great Robhurst, Woodchurch, Ashford, Kent TN26 3TB, England
Unsolicited manuscripts are considered for publication in *New Theatre Quarterly*. They should be sent to Simon Trussler at the above address, but unless accompanied by a stamped addressed envelope (UK stamp or international reply coupons) return cannot be guaranteed. Contributors are asked to follow the journal's house style as closely as possible.

Subscriptions
New Theatre Quarterly (ISSN: 0266-464X) is published quarterly by Cambridge University Press, The Edinburgh Building, Shaftesbury Road, Cambridge CB2 2RU, UK, and The Journals Department, 40 West 20th Street, New York, NY 10011-4211, USA.

Four parts form a volume. The subscription price, which includes postage (excluding VAT), of Volume XIII, 1997, is £47.00 (US$82.00 in the USA, Canada and Mexico) for institutions, £27.00 (US$39.00) for individuals ordering direct from the publishers and certifying that the Journal is for their personal use. Single parts cost £13.00 (US$22.00 in the USA, Canada and Mexico) plus postage. EU subscribers (outside the UK) who are not registered for VAT should add VAT at their country's rate. VAT registered subscribers should provide their VAT registration number. Prices include delivery by air. Japanese prices for institutions are available from Kinokuniya Company Ltd., P.O. Box 55, Chitose, Tokyo 156, Japan.

Orders, which must be accompanied by payment, may be sent to a bookseller or to the publishers (in the USA, Canada and Mexico to the North American Branch). Periodicals postage paid at New York, NY, and at additional mailing offices. POSTMASTER: send address changes in the USA, Canada and Mexico to *New Theatre Quarterly*, Cambridge University Press, The Journals Department, 40 West 20th Street, New York, NY 10011-4211.

Claims for missing issues will only be considered if made immediately on receipt of the following issue.

Information on *New Theatre Quarterly* and all other Cambridge journals can be accessed via http://www.cup.cam.ac.uk/ and in North America via http://www.cup.org/.

The Edinburgh Building, Cambridge CB2 2RU, United Kingdom
40 West 20th Street, New York, NY 10011-4211, USA
10 Stamford Road, Oakleigh, Melbourne 3166, Australia

Typeset by Country Setting, Woodchurch, Ashford, Kent TN26 3TB
Printed and bound in the United Kingdom at the University Press, Cambridge

Maria Shevtsova

Resistance and Resilience: an Overview of the Maly Theatre of St Petersburg

The reputation of the Maly Theatre of St Petersburg has been growing steadily in this country and elsewhere – ironically, since the economic problems of its native Russia have made touring as much a matter of economic necessity as of cultural cross-fertilization. In the following article, Maria Shevtsova offers a detailed explication of four of the Maly's most notable productions under its present director, Lev Dodin – Aleksandr Galin's *Stars in the Morning Sky*, appropriately one of the final offerings within the ambit of the former Soviet Union; *Brothers and Sisters*, a view of a Russia in 'perpetual motion' in the immediate post-war years which has come to be regarded as the company's 'signature piece'; a transposition onto the stage of Dostoevsky's masterpiece, *The Devils*; and – following briefer studies of G*audeamus* and *Claustrophobia* – a revival of *The Cherry Orchard* which, like so much of Dodin's work, offers a bleak vision of disintegration as Chekhov's portrayal of a crumbling society at the turn of the last century comes full circle to reflect our own *fin de siècle*. Maria Shevtsova is Professor of Contemporary Performance and Theatre Studies at the University of Lancaster, and has published on a wide range of subjects including the work of Peter Brook, Ariane Mnouchkine, Patrice Chéreau, and Robert Wilson, having also contributed a three-part study of 'The Sociology of Theatre' to NTQ17-19 (1989). Her most recent full-length work is *Theatre and Cultural Interaction* (1993).

WHEN the Maly Theatre directed by Lev Dodin first performed in Britain in 1988 at the Glasgow Mayfest and the Riverside Studios in London, it brought *Stars in the Morning Sky*, a play by Aleksandr Galin set in the outskirts of Moscow during the Olympics of 1980. The production had been in the Maly's repertoire since 1987, when it was shown in Leningrad and Moscow after several months of altercation with the authorities. Gorbachev had been in power for a little over a year, and, although the state apparatus still controlled the arts, the spirit of reconstruction and openness – perestroika and glasnost – was already strong enough to conquer censorship. Arguably, indeed, the Soviet government and the Communist Party were anticipating some sort of meltdown that Lev Dodin and his company must also have sensed when, seemingly against all odds, they persisted with their venture.

Audiences in the then-Soviet Union were more or less aware of how beggars, drunks, and prostitutes had been shunted out of sight to the Moscow periphery in order to keep the streets 'clean' for the Olympic Games. They reeled, nevertheless, from the shock of a production that not only tackled the subject head on, but did so with a brutality and violence unprecedented in their theatre.

The production's boldness foregrounds a tale about the enforced cohabitation of four prostitutes, among them a fifteen-year-old mother, in a dilapidated shack that usually housed the inmates of a mental hospital nearby. The caretaker of the hospital oversees the women. Meanwhile, her militia son falls in love with the minor, who is as good as gang-raped by her clients. One of the other women makes tender love with a wandering patient from the hospital, their couple and coupling giving images of purity and holy idiocy worthy of a Dostoevsky. Notwithstanding its beauty, the nudity of the love scene was, by sheer dint of its novelty, as startling to spectators as the emotional, verbal, and environmental coarseness which, by turns funny and horrific, was represented for them.

Reactions – and Returns

The reaction from the press in Britain was muted as regards the production's provocative character – not surprisingly, of course, given the greater threshold of tolerance to artistic liberty in this country. What had attracted attention, rather, was the *significance* of such direct interference in the mechanisms of repression and control. Thus, for example, *Financial Times* critic Michael Coveney perceived the whole production as a 'cultural symptom of glasnost' (11 May 1988).

Some confined its importance to the Soviet Union/Russia. Most felt compelled to connect glasnost, Galin's play, and Dodin's production in some way to Britain. Their purpose was to assert, as *The Observer* put it, 'the common humanity between all the characters and between them and us', and yet, at the same time, indicate that cultural differences give rise to theatrical differences, which contradict ideas as to how everything everywhere is the same. *The Observer*, consequently, also noted that 'this is a theatre of passion and consolation: it could be American or Irish, but it would be unlikely to have come out of England today'.

The Independent took up the twin themes of commonality and difference by stating that 'this fruit of glasnost' from the Maly 'must be shatteringly brave in Russia, but its courage is instructive here too'. The courage invoked concerned the material performed (taken, in the British context, to be 'the underside of image-conscious society') as well as the manner of performing it ('fine passionate performances') – both of which explained, according to *The Independent*, why the Maly 'blasts away some of the confines in which what passes for theatre can operate'. As these statements show, the Maly was seen to provide several 'instructive' models, social and theatrical, in one.

Still on the issue of 'them and us', *The Guardian* alluded to the temptation to react to Galin's play 'with a kind of smug, back-patting response, as though it were all about the Soviets, under glasnost, acquiring the same freedom as us to write rude plays about nasty subjects like prostitution, alcoholism and sexual violence'. The review concluded with reference to the old prostitute Anna (Tatyana Shestakova), who is seen to be 'the symbol of humanity in the modern age, selling itself for bread, and finding its whole life shaped by forces it barely begins to understand'.

The Financial Times shared this global point of view: 'The play tells you much about Russia, but even more about the world.' The company it described simply as 'wonderful'. *Stars in the Morning Sky* received an Olivier Award, an honour that acknowledged, whatever political implications it harboured, the production's impact on theatre professionals and general theatre-goers alike.

All these observations suggest that critics in Britain were likely to be favourably predisposed towards the Maly on its further visits in 1990, 1991, and 1992, and even how they may have sensitized audiences to the company's work. On these occasions, the Maly brought its phenomenal epic *Brothers and Sisters*. The 1991 tour also included the London International Festival of Theatre, which hosted *Gaudeamus*, a production that had been performed in Germany in the previous year. What was singled out for particular attention on these occasions was the 'beautiful ensemble work' – as *The Times* summed up the overall critical response.

When the Maly came on its fifth tour in 1994, this refrain recurred again and again – rightly so, moreover. Irrespective of their newspapers' presumed politics or their own personal foibles, the critics referred variously to the 'ensemble movement', to 'ensemble acting', an 'exceptional ensemble', an 'ensemble like no other', the 'legendary ensemble skills of the Maly', and so on, each variant of the consensus accompanied by superlatives for specific details of this or that performance.

The 1994 tour was billed as a retrospective, and was indeed a mammoth event.

It comprised five productions running over seven weeks in five cities (Glasgow, Newcastle, Manchester, Nottingham, London). It was also part of a larger European tour that kept the Maly away from St Petersburg for nearly six months. The productions were *Brothers and Sisters* (six hours in two parts), *The House* (four hours), *Stars in the Morning Sky* (approximately two and a half hours without intermission), *The Devils* (eight hours in three parts), and *The Cherry Orchard* (two and a half hours without intermission).

Over eighty company members were involved in the tour, *Brothers and Sisters* alone taking forty people, thirty and more of them being on stage at any one time. The sheer size and scope of the enterprise, the daring of the programming (in view, for instance, of the unfamiliarity to British audiences of most of the material presented) and the focus, concentration, and stamina required for such long and demanding performances are some indication of the Maly's human, creative, and organizational capabilities. To grasp the full scale of the endeavour, one should add to the Maly's various expenditures the considerable financial outlay and managerial effort and coordination on the part of the theatres and cities welcoming it.

A sixth visit occurred in 1996. During this *Gaudeamus* was showcased, as well as *Claustrophobia* which had been premiered in Paris in 1994. Both productions had been part of the 1994 European tour, but had not been shown then in Britain. A seventh visit is planned for 1998.

Dodin's 'Theatre of Prose'

Brothers and Sisters, which by now could well be described as the Maly's signature piece, grew out of a long process of work with students of acting taught by Dodin and Arkady Katzman at the St Petersburg Academy of Theatre Arts (formerly the Leningrad Theatre Institute), where Dodin himself had graduated in 1967. Dodin and Katzman (who has since died) adapted the script from Fedor Abramov's trilogy *The Chronicles of Pekashino*, which was published between 1968 and 1972. This novel was a milestone in what was known in the 'seventies as 'peasant' or 'village literature', the genre either extolling the virtues of village life, and idealizing it in the process, or focusing on its many difficulties so as to produce, all the more stridently, optimistic visions of the future.

Abramov made his native Verkola in the Arkhangelsk region the model for Pekashino, showing how its harsh conditions and deprivations were typical of those rural communities whose sacrifices for the country's good, particularly in the hungry years immediately after the Second World War, went virtually unrewarded and ended up, in fact, as severe penalties. He thereby called into question the official, 'optimistic' ideology on collective farms or *kolkhoz* that had reigned in the Soviet Union since Stalin's collectivization programme in the 'thirties.

Abramov was a communist, which did not prevent him from running into trouble over his critique. He died in 1983, but not before he had seen several experimental versions of his book devised by Academy students. Dodin subsequently reworked the 1978 student production that had emerged, opening in 1985 the 'final' version for professional theatre that is performed today.

It must be noted, along with this brief account of the sources of *Brothers and Sisters*, that most of the Maly actors are graduates of the St Petersburg Academy. Many of them who are now in their late forties and early fifties were contemporaries of Dodin at this outstanding school. Those who are in their late thirties were trained in the 'seventies by Dodin and Katzman. With one or two exceptions, they now play the same roles in *Brothers and Sisters* that they had developed during their student days.

The youngest members of the company are from Dodin's class at the Academy in the 'eighties. Then there are the actors in *Gaudeamus* and *Claustrophobia*, most of whom are his present 'trainees' (the rest of the cast are older company members). This team of brilliant apprentices runs parallel with the Maly Drama Theatre, but does not yet have the status of a professional company as such. Dodin, like Stanislavsky before him, works on the principle that a theatre school and a theatre company must mutually nurture each other, the interrelationship between pedagogical processes, artistic research, and performance providing the best conditions possible for creativity. The Maly's ensemble power, which has been celebrated enthusiastically, even ecstatically, throughout the world, owes a great deal to the Stanislavskian school–company foundations on which the Maly has evolved its practice at every level of its operations.

Brothers and Sisters has, then, a special place in the Maly repertoire for what might be called historical as well as emblematic reasons. It was not, however, Dodin's first large-scale production, but was preceded in 1980 by *The House* – also an adaptation of a novel by Abramov, his fourth in the Pekashino series, which was published in 1978. *The House*, in other words, is anomolous from a chronological point of view in that its stage existence precedes *Brothers and Sisters*, whereas its narrative logic follows it.

Brothers and Sisters covers the years from 1945 to 1950. *The House* takes up the thread of Pekashino life in the 1960s. The fact that the pieces were prepared in different circumstances – *Brothers and Sisters* with students and *The House* with the company – helps explain why different actors play the same characters who appear in both. Since, strictly speaking, these productions were not conceived in tandem, they can be seen separately without any loss of sense. When seen together, however, they form a vast fresco where huge public events and small domestic incidents intertwine, and this with a finesse and potency perhaps comparable only to Tolstoy's *War and Peace*.

Whether taken together or separately, they are superb examples of devised theatre and especially of the kind that Dodin calls the 'theatre of prose' – of which *The Devils* is another example, and a comparatively very recent one. An adaptation of the novel by Dostoevsky, it was premiered in Braunschweig in Germany in 1991.

The Cherry Orchard, which appears last in the list of productions on tour given above, is the first of what promises to be a Chekhov cycle. It had its beginnings in a two-week international workshop held in the Borders in 1993. The production was commissioned by the Odéon-Théâtre de l'Europe in Paris, where it opened in 1994. The Maly is currently rehearsing Chekhov's first play – untitled, but generally known as *Platonov* – and this will open in Weimar in 1997.

The Contemporary Repertoire

The Maly Drama Theatre was founded in 1944 at the tail end of the seige of Leningrad, whose horrors might well have ruled out any thought of anyone starting a new theatre at all. Dodin became the Maly's artistic director in 1983 after having assised Efim Padve, its former director, from 1975. He also continued to occupy the teaching position at the Academy of Theatre Arts he still holds today. Ten Dodin productions now alternate in repertory. Among them, beside the five already cited, are shows from the Anglo-American canon, notably, *The Rose Tattoo*, *Desire Under the Elms*, and a 'theatre of prose' version of *Lord of the Flies*.

Gaudeamus and *Claustrophbia*, although performed alternately with the others, are considered to belong to the student ensemble. The first of these is a hilarious piece in nineteen sequences loosely based on *The Construction Battalion*, a satirical novel of 1988 by Sergei Kaledin on the squalor and disintegration within the Soviet army. The second is devised from improvisations by the young performers on their impressions of Russia after their return from touring abroad. The 1991 *coup d'état* virtually meant that they had left one country and returned to another.

What must also be noted here are the two productions in collaboration with the Odéon-Théâtre de l'Europe that are not so much a matter of cross-cultural exploration as of institutional linkage – as well as of professional–personal novelty and enrichment. The first of these is *Roberto Zucco*, the last play by the self-defined outcast Bernard-Marie Koltès before his death in 1989. This was staged by Luis Pasqual in 1994, with the

Maly actors performing in Russian both in Paris and St Petersburg. Pasqual was then director of the Odéon on the five-year term prescribed by this state-subsidized theatre. The production allowed him simultaneously to pay homage to Koltès and to fulfil an old dream to work with Russian actors – the Maly company never having worked with any director other than Dodin before. The second production to come out of the collaborative venture was *Reflets*, staged in 1996 by the Odéon's present director Georges Lavaudant (with text by Lavaudant and the currently visible writers Jean-Christophe Bailly, Michel Deutsch, and Jean-François Duroure).

Aspects of the Maly Methodology

The Maly's working processes are possibly unique in theatre today. There is, first of all, the interconnection between the school for actors as such, the performances mounted through the research of these apprentices, the ongoing research through retreats and similar gatherings of the company members, and the established repertoire. This system encourages growth and regeneration, and allows the Maly to explore the achievements of the Russian theatre since Stanislavsky and Meyerhold – not merely to rediscover or recover them, but to take them into new directions and find a path that is very much its own. Further, it pushes beyond the insights of such past luminaries, and realizes these insights in ways that were neither conceivable nor technically possible in previous decades – such, for example, would be the case with what Stanislavsky thought of as 'physical actions' or what Meyerhold understood by 'carrying through' movement.

Secondly, Maly productions take shape gradually after long periods of gestation in which everyone is involved – performers, a literary adviser *cum* translator/interpreter, and other assistants, stage and costume designers, and voice, dance, and music teachers. However, productions are not permanently set in stone once they have acquired their form, but continue to mature through performances at home and abroad.

From this follows the third noteworthy point, which is touring. Touring aids the process of maturation which the Maly believes is essential for artistic quality. In addition, despite its stresses, time-warps, cultural dislocation, and unhinging, touring provides opportunities like no other for seeing and reviewing work in a different light and developing it accordingly.

This is not to ignore the imperative to tour internationally imposed on the Maly by the collapse of state subsidies. How else, indeed, if not through touring and the commissions, invitations, professional exchanges and possibilities for outside funding, all of which are tied up with the touring network, does such a large company survive? How, apart from the question of its size, does a group of people so deeply committed to an accumulative process of work actually sustain its working principles? My point is that, although touring brings in some money to help the Maly work, it is not undertaken merely for financial reasons. Touring, with its demands on people's resourcefulness, also suits the *way* the Maly works.

The fourth point to note is the importance of devising. There is the devising from prose fiction, which, as was indicated for *Brothers and Sisters*, is far more than a matter of writing a script. Thus, performances are not tailored to a text but crafted out of numerous exercises, improvisations, experiments, sketches, notions, or simply intuitions. The various kinds of 'drafts' for productions that emerge from these activities can be inspired by a particular text, or be based on ideas or scenes from it.

Devising also relies on what might be called the more spontaneous modes – sensations, streams of consciousness, unrestrained word play, body play, mime, mimicry, and clowning, among others. *Claustrophobia* thus grew out of this 'free-form' approach to devising and incorporated it in its aesthetic. And although other Maly productions were not constructed from free-form elements, as happened with *Claustrophobia*, all of them, including *The Cherry Orchard*, used free-form procedures at one stage or another of their preparation and evolution.

Fifthly, the Maly practises a particular kind of ecological theatre. By this I am referring to how, for *Brothers and Sisters*, the company spent long periods working in the village, woods, and monastery of Abramov's Verkola, or how, for *The Cherry Orchard*, time was spent in the Sakhalin peninsula, where Chekhov had worked as a doctor. The aim was to be immersed in these natural as well as social environments so as to store their rhythms in the muscles and nerves and then subsequently to draw on this body memory for performance. The indispensability of body memory is brought home, in *Brothers and Sisters*, by how the actors' posture, gait, movements, and gestures – in short, their whole kinesics individually and in relation to each other – give their characters a three-dimensional plasticity that far exceeds a merely well-observed, realistic-picture portrayal.

By the same token, immersion in the Verkola environment allows them to speak the Archangelsk dialect required by the production with ease and even to capture the differentiation by gender in speech – the women of this northern region speaking with a rather sing-song intonation while the men's diction hardens consonants and cadences. These local distinctions are very important for a production that accentuates, as does Abramov, the role of peasant women in keeping the entire country going both during the Second World War and in the years of reconstruction straight after it.

The drawback for non-Russian speakers is that they are bound to miss the nuances implied by the vernacular – a normal loss not just of semantic but cultural meaning when one moves to a foreign language. Even so, the production's care with sound patterns warns spectators that they are quite significant, the sonic differences to do with gender probably being the most accessible to the ear.

'Brothers and Sisters' as a Matrix

What follows are selected analytical details from *Brothers and Sisters*, *The Devils*, and *The Cherry Orchard*, as well as *Gaudeamus* and *Claustrophobia*, the two productions of the student ensemble. The purpose is to give a general though not imprecise view of the Maly's richly varied performance style. Emphasis will be placed on *Brothers and Sisters* and to a lesser extent on *The Cherry Orchard*.

The first piece requires special attention because of its important role in the Maly's history. It is also something of a matrix for the rest. Since the ground it covers is not familiar, a story outline of the production will be helpful. The second is a new point of departure. Not only does it presage a Chekhov cycle, but is the company's first production under Dodin's leadership of a Russian *dramatic* classic, as distinct from a prose classic like *The Devils*. (In any case, even where prose is concerned, the Maly privileges contemporary writing concerned with contemporary issues.)

Furthermore, instead of devising its own playscript, the Maly here interprets a pre-existing text. So far, *Stars in the Morning Sky* has been the only other Russian play performed by the Maly. In addition, with *The Cherry Orchard*, the company faces the peculiar challenges to insight and ingenuity offered by a work that has been performed so frequently that it can no longer be extricated from the multiple interpretations and reinterpretations encrusted upon it.

Part One of *Brothers and Sisters*, which is made up of two acts, begins with a collage of oral and aural images. Transcending all is Stalin's famous 1941 speech in which he roused the Soviet people to battle to crush the nazi enemy – and which opened with the address 'brothers and sisters' that gave the production its title. Film extracts of the war and of returning soldiers being greeted with kisses and flowers appear on a screen of logs which suggests the wall of a peasant hut or izba. This heavy screen swings up to reveal a crowd of villagers who soon surge forward as if to welcome their own heroes (although, as becomes clear, only one out of sixty men returns).

More villagers enter through the audience, among them two running children. There is noise, chatter, laughter, movement, and dance. Several men bring in piles of hay, and two younger men, Misha and Egorsha, arrive after having spent the winter in the forest cutting timber for the State. It is spring 1945. The quick flashes back to the immediate past firmly anchor the time, place, and cultural space of the story about to unfold. Most of its protagonists are in the huge crowd on stage. All are important, and even the smallest roles are shown to be essential to the texture of the whole.

Interweaving of People and Politics

However, a number of these protagonists are the narrative's main references. They are Misha, his mother Anna and sister Lizka, Egorsha, Varvara, Anfisa, and Ganichev. Two more characters who are indispensible to the plot, Grigory and Pershin, appear in the second act. Misha is barely out of his adolescence, but is the head of a family of five children, his father having been killed during the war. He will soon lose his closest friend Egorsha, who will seek work in town. Misha and Varvara fall in love and have a sexual relationship. She is a war widow who is older than Misha and who is accused by the villagers of having seduced him. Varvara is disgraced and ordered to leave the collective farm by Anfisa, its chief.

Anfisa's husband Grigory, who had been presumed missing, returns unexpectedly. Anfisa tells him she cannot forget how he had beaten her and can no longer be his wife. She is waiting for the return of Ivan with whom she fell in love when he was convalescing in Pekashino after a war injury. Grigory and Varvara run off to the town together – this part of the plot being reported by one of the villagers when Misha is lumbering in the forest. Ganichev, the district chief, deplores the poor economic results of the *kolkhoz* and, blaming Anfisa for them, proposes that Pershin, a former army officer, replace her. The *kolkhoz* workers cast their votes against Anfisa. Misha is her most vociferous opponent because he cannot forgive her for breaking up his relationship with Varvara.

Part Two is also in two acts. Its opening moments echo the opening of Part One, the difference being that the images projected this time are in colour and from a propaganda film of the 'fifties on the successes of collective farming. Five years have now passed. Anfisa and Ivan are married, and Ivan is the new president of the *kolkhoz*. Numerous details which complicate the story have to do with the economic ruin of Pekashino – the way the men are sent to lumber camps in the forest, and are thus forced to neglect the farm; how the machinery is old and broken; how the roof of a recently constructed stable is left unfinished because the men building it are fed up with not being paid, even in kind; how the women continue to work hard, sowing and reaping and doing numerous other tasks; how the harvests are taken away from them by the State for distribution elsewhere.

Then there is a campaign for borrowing money from the villagers, who resist handing over their paltry savings; accusations of malingering against the returned soldier who had been imprisoned in a concentration camp and who eventually takes himself to the hospital in town where he dies of cancer; hunger, fatigue, and discussions on where the fault lies for the *kolkhoz*'s ruin – in the devastation caused by the war or in the politics of the State.

The tableaux foregrounding major public issues are constantly overlaid by personal events. Egorsha comes back to the village with news of better economic conditions in town. He flirts with Lizka. Their marriage takes place in the second act. Here, too, personal decisions become political ones. Ivan, who is appalled by how the men abandon the stable roof so as to unload a river steam ship for goods as payment, decides to give each of them a fifteen-kilo bag of grain.

His intended action is illegal. Egorsha stops the bags from being distributed. The district authorities hear of the incident and arrest Ivan. Misha asks the villagers to sign a letter in Ivan's defence. All refuse, except for Lizka, whom Egorsha forbids to sign. She does so, nevertheless, arguing that living without a conscience is worse than not living at all. Egorsha leaves her. Meanwhile,

Anfisa has met Varvara in town and learns that she still grieves over Misha. Misha, like Lizka, ends *Brothers and Sisters* on a high moral note, but his life in pieces.

A Principle of Perpetual Motion

This bare-bones account of the production's story and content may make it sound morose, and, at worst, like a merely subversive variation upon a 'wooden' socialist realist model. Or, again, it may appear to be little more than a retake of such famous tough–delicate post-war films as *The Cranes are Flying* – to which there are some fairly unobtrusive allusions, including the filmic framing, travelling and jump-cuts of certain scenes and especially of the first scenes of Part One.

Yet none of these possible impressions corresponds with what actually happens on stage. The production's aesthetic is based on a principle of perpetual motion, on currents of action which pull together the discrete units – tableaux, sections, fragments, codas – into a composition of symphonic depth and line and also of an extraordinarily infectious joyfulness. The whole gives the illusion that time and motion have no beginning or end, and, for the spectators who are willing to go with it, it takes them into another spatio-temporal dimension altogether. The effect is one of simplicity and effortlessness, which is also a matter of *trompe l'oeil* in that the theatrical styling demands from the actors complete control over their vocal, gestural, and kinesic skills.

These features are the basis of that fine ensemble acting which earned the Maly critical acclaim worldwide. The ease of the actors allows them to play mass scenes in which over thirty characters may appear together and perform whatever actions are required without making them too 'busy', or 'stagey' or 'operatic' in the worst senses of these words. Ceremonial scenes such as the end of the first act of Part One, for example, are a particularly testing case in point.

Here a party is held in honour of the first soldier who has returned from the war. The party is created in full view as the actors mill around and set up tables, covering them with white cloth, flowers, bottles, and food. Someone brings in a red flag. Someone else plays an accordion while others chat, sing, or mark out dance steps here and there. Toasts are given to victory, to the women who had maintained the farm, and to the motherland (and in a later, parallel scene also to Stalin) without any snide overtones, although the players and audience know perfectly well how badly history turned out. In this, as in other areas open to (superior) irony, the production places the dignity of its characters above the egos of its makers.

The occasion is brought about at top speed, its pace hiding the fact that it has all been finely orchestrated. And the actors are so entirely focused on what they are doing that these ordinary actions look quite natural – though certainly not naturalistic, which is a technique that, by attempting to make actions meaningful, only succeeds in making them banal. The scene is also built on contrasts and shadings. The great upsurge of noise and of movement suddenly subsides as everybody concentrates solely on the sheer bliss of eating. For several split seconds there is absolute silence, though it does not go dead since everyone is visibly, albeit quietly, eating. Then there is an explosion of laughter, talk, kissing, dancing, witty ditties (*chastushki*), folk songs sung in descant, and too much vodka – the whole drawing explicitly on Russian rural culture so as to give the dramatic action its full social and emotional value.

All these different activities are carried out at their own tempo. Above all, they are carried through without interruption as some merge with or are replaced by others. The flow of time, pace, and movement also allows larger transitions to occur seamlessly, as happens in the course of the party where Misha and Varvara dance together and fall in love. And a similar flow resurges more strongly still towards the very end of Part One, when a scene featuring Misha and Egorsha turns without interruption into a scene for Misha and Varvara who, for no apparent reason other than that events

Youthful flirtation and neighbourly affection in the Maly Theatre's production of *Brothers and Sisters*, with (top) Sergei Vlasov as Egorsha and Natalia Fomenko as Varvara. Photos: Maly Drama Theatre.

merge into each other, comes through a door at centre stage. She walks towards Misha, who lifts her up to the sounds of the victory march that had opened the production some three hours before.

Varvara (Natalia Fomenko) is a stunning, tall beauty with braids around her head like a crown. Misha's mother and siblings appear from nowhere, as also does a table covered in white, and several women bring ribbons and bread, which is cut by a man in uniform who resembles a portrait of Misha's father. More women run in as soldiers pour in through the audience. Wheat and flakes of light fall like confetti on the crowd. The music plays on as a radiant happiness envelopes all.

The audience has come to realize that two major events have converged: one is the return of the soldiers, which was celebrated by the party earlier on, and the other is a wedding feast. The party, moreover, is the initial point of departure for diverse scenes that flow on, like one long stream with its different tributaries, until they eventually culminate in this feast. But spectators will discover at the beginning of the second act that this magnificent celebration is a wish-fantasy, an exteriorization of Varvara and Misha's desire which is so compelling that they, just like the other protagonists, are swept up by it and taken out of normal time into the time of day-dreams. Also, the dead return alive in this other time, as does, in Misha's imagination, his father with the other soldiers who had perished during the war. New Age 'go with the flow' could hardly ask for a more transcendental experience.

Metaphor, Humour, and Juxtaposition

Two more examples of ensemble interaction will show how the Maly's performance style relies on metaphoric, poetic levels of expression. The first involves the women sowing early in Part One. The other concerns both women and men working in the forest, and occurs closer towards the end of the same part. From a compositional point of view, the two scenes are echoes, in different registers, of each other. Light is used in both to create a setting. It is also a doubling device in that it completes and repeats actors' actions.

In the women's scene, for instance, scattered light duplicates the image of showers of seeds sent across a field. The performers, in the meantime, sing in harmony, swing their arms wide in unison and stomp their feet forward as they sow – their piece, for all its cohesion, managing to avoid a chorus-line effect. In the forest scene, sheets of yellow light suggest the sun coming through trees, alternately obscuring the performers, as if they were blending into the shadows of trees, and throwing their silhouettes into relief. By the same token, the use of sheeting conjures up images of falling logs – the visual complement and 'result' of the actors' actions. The relative silence of the forest evoked here contrasts with the noise of the women lying around on the floor in a large cluster and telling dirty jokes between sowing. The cluster of bodies is an effective metaphor in itself for the sense of ensemble established.

The easy changes from place to place are made possible by an ingenious piece of decor designed by Eduard Kochergin: the log platform that serves as a film-screen at the beginning of Parts One and Two, and which can be swung to any height and set virtually at any angle. Its metaphoric capacity is boundless. It can represent a field or forest, and be used accordingly at floor level. It may hang as a roof for a bath house, or tilt to become a grain-chute or a truck on which bags of grain are loaded. It can be stood erect to become the inner wall of a room or the outer wall of a hut. It can be laid out to give the angle of a street or a court-yard. Or it can be lifted to designate various spaces – among these the hay loft where Varvara and Misha make love.

It also hides secrets, such as the trapdoor that spectators are to imagine in the loft floor when Anfisa hounds the lovers. This particular sketch is extremely funny in that the timing of Anfisa's harangues is impeccable and her expressions nothing less than silly as she looks and talks into thin air rather than in the lovers' direction. The vignette exploits a range of fairly standard comic effects in order to mock them playfully and, in this way, emphasizes the theatricality of the moment rather than its narrative, emotional, or any other significance. The impact comes only afterwards from the contrast between this highly performed, highly theatricalized event and its profound human consequences.

Humour is a constant feature of *Brothers and Sisters*, despite its dark undertow. It animates cameos, as happens when Anfisa tries on the patent black high-heels that Grigory brings her – citified objects that are quite incongruous with her peasant dress. It has a satirical thrust at particular points, as happens when an authoritarian voice can be heard barking down a telephone to Ganichev on his rounds of the farm. Or, again, it may run right through extended sequences – as happens in Part Two when Egorsha visits the village.

The sound of a roaring motorbike prepares the audience for the appearance of a cocky, macho boy-from-town, who is none the less infinitely likeable – ensuring that all the laughs at Egorsha's expense are good-natured and affectionate. Egorsha is also very seductive in a youthful, fresh sort of way. Lizka, for all her awkward shoes and buckets, is no less open or charming.

The conclusive phase of their flirtation takes place on the edge of the stage and is filled with details (including Egorsha's bandaged thumb, which he sports ridiculously for sympathy without getting it) that, on the one hand, show how they come closer together, physically and emotionally, and, on the other, entice the audience to share in their comic game. For instance, Lizka's legs dangle casually, which is deceptive given her swift reactions to Egorsha's amorous attacks – while Egorsha's angelic demeanour contradicts the fierce sexuality of his manoeuvres.

The cluster of juxtapositions constituting this sequence follows a general principle of juxtaposition working through the production by which sequences are identified as well as distinguished from each other – the most pronounced being the distinction between Lizka and Egorsha's delightful play for love and Varvara and Misha's intoxicating, tenacious passion.

Scenography and Mise-en-Scène

My preceding paragraphs have drawn attention to the symbiosis in *Brothers and Sisters* between Kochergin's scenography and Dodin's mise en scène. It is now important to refer to Kochergin's design for *The Devils*, which may well prove to be the crowning achievement of his collaboration with the director since *The House* in 1980. It is equally important to look at the sets of *Gaudeamus* and *Claustrophobia*. These are the work of Alexei Porai-Koshits, who also designed *Stars in the Morning Sky*. The main purpose of these cross-references, however brief, is to point out that one of the fundamental aspects of Dodin's work as a director is his exploration of space. What this means more precisely is that he explores the way performers may *inhabit* space and, concomitantly, how far they can be stretched as *performers* by the kinds of space they use.

Kochergin's design for *Brothers and Sisters* allows Dodin to pursue his goal of turning a proscenium arch into a flexible space. A similar intention for *The Devils* meets with a far more radical solution. *Brothers and Sisters* gives Dodin some loopholes: after all, the log platform can be positioned in ways that open up space. Here there are no loopholes, in that Kochergin's design determines all the parameters of the mise en scène.

The space, moreover, has the closeness of a maze. Thus Dodin's direction relies entirely on a series of wooden plank-pulleys that swivel, heave, and lift by means of ropes, and that turn sideways or at an angle or fall flat, usually two or three moving at a time. The sense of danger conveyed through these movements is intensified through how they also form narrow see-saws on which the actors walk and run. The whole construction plunges downwards to what would normally be the space below the stage. This underground is essential for the continuity of movement, wherever it begins or ends, whether in the underground itself, on the stage, on a surface suspended above the stage, in the wings – or, as happens frequently (and especially in Part Two) on the sides of the stage or right on the ground, level with the audience.

What would be the walls of the stage are black. The construction set in them shows us the nooks and crannies, the streets, bridges, canals, and slums, and all the tight, airless rooms of Dostoevsky's St Petersburg. This is a forbidding, brooding place from whose secret crevices emerge Dostoevsky-Dodin's possessed. They are revolutionaries and/or nihilsts, atheists and/or supermen, and manipulators and power-mongers of all kinds. Among them are women crazed by poverty, abuse, and suffering.

The actors play their characters with an uncanny intensity of focus. They appear or disappear abruptly, or fade in or out of view like ghosts. Or else they relentlessly pursue their prey, physically and psychologically, through the maze of beams and planks, going up or down, now visible, now not, depending on the sight-lines of the maze. Such is the pursuit of Stavrogin, Dostoevsky's arch manipulator (played by Peter Semak, Misha in *Brothers and Sisters*, whose role transformation is staggering). Such is Verkhovensky's search for Kirillov, whom he finally hunts down and coolly persuades to take his own life – his suicide to prove that God did not exist and could not exist when human beings asserted their supremacy through acts of will that contested divine power.

Actors, Roles, and the 'Great Idea'

Dodin's grandiose project of transposing Dostoevsky onto the stage is commensurate only with his ambition for his actors. What becomes absolutely clear, especially when a spectator is able to observe the production's evolution over a number of years (including its development in St Petersburg, where the work has a particular resonance for actors and audience alike), is how, by fully inhabiting the space of their characters, the actors finish up by possessing them entirely, intimating the somatic fusion between actor and character sought by Stanislavky. By stretching themselves so far that all boundaries of play seem to disappear, the actors surpass their previous achievements, thus reaching another higher, technical and emotional plane.

This transformative process doesn't seem to end with acting *per se*, since the actors appear to undergo an enormous ontological experience that affects their identity as people. One might need here to speak of a process of merging where actor and person become one, despite the fact that the actor playing a character must let go of that character in 'real life' at some point.

Something else becomes clearer with time, and that is the secret, subliminal link between *The Devils* and *Brothers and Sisters*. *Brothers and Sisters* could be described as the pursuit, by human beings, of a grand idea. *The Devils* reverses this proposition: an idea, which becomes the Great Idea, here pursues human beings relentlessly until it consumes them. The clue to this encoded message about possession lies in the scene where Verkhovensky voraciously consumes a chicken, bones and all, while subtly driving Kirillov to his death.

The scene is chilling, sickening even – particularly when spectators remember that there were times in Russia, not as far back as the post-war years of *Brothers and Sisters*, let alone Dostoevsky's time, when finding a chicken, let alone imagining that one person could gobble it up, was simply unthinkable. The actor who plays Verkhovensky (Sergei Bekhterev, who performs Gaev in *The Cherry Orchard*) eats with a contemptuous greed that offsets his cold and steely performance throughout.

The last, demonic encounter between Verkhovensky and the Kirillov of Sergei Kurishev (who plays Trofimov in *The Cherry Orchard*) produces acting of such concentration and limpidity that it is utterly riveting. If it could be said that the whole of the twentieth century in European theatre has been a search for perfection in the art of acting, the Verkhovensky–Kirillov scene here must surely be one of the high peaks of this quest.

Top: from the Maly production of *Gaudeamus* (photo: Ken Reynolds). Bottom: from the Maly adaptation of Dostoevsky's *The Devils* (photo: Maly Drama Theatre).

Let us now turn to *Gaudeamus* and then to *Claustrophobia*. We have seen how, in *The Devils*, Dodin and his actors use space below the stage in order to explore ways of articulating fine, inner movements of heart and mind and the motivations for behaviour. This includes what might be described as the psychology of fanaticism. In *Gaudeamus*, the equivalent space is used for developing acrobatic skills purely for external action. The genre is now comedy of the most explicit, direct kind.

Playing with Music and Movement

The design by Porai-Kochits is startlingly simple, with the stage covered in white to give an impression of snow. Spectators realize that there are rows of small trapdoors in the floor of the stage only when these are popped open by the actors who appear from beneath. They soon discover that the doors lead to the latrines that the Red Army has been assigned to keep clean. The actors slide, glide, jump, or disappear head first into them. Acrobatic agility, rhythmic precision, and speed and timing are exploited for a series of side-splitting incidents, some being pure burlesque, others wicked satire.

All sorts of surprises are devised to keep the actors alert and their audiences laughing. There are, for example, brass instruments which are thrown up by invisible hands out of the black holes of the traps. This surprise is followed by another when the actors not only catch the large instruments but, in one unbroken movement, put them to their lips and play jazz. At the same time, more actors playing trombones, trumpets, and horns burst forth from the trapdoors.

The fact that they actually play these instruments, rather than play with them as objects, is calculated to astonish. The fact that they play them so well causes even more astonishment, not to mention delight. Later in the performance a shower of matchboxes pours out through the holes. These contain each soldier's excrement, supposedly for testing. At this point the stage is empty, and the sight of jumping boxes full of shit sums up the state of the army.

What should become clear from these examples is the discipline, virtuosity, and versatility of Dodin's student actors. Not only are they supposed to clamber out of the holes quickly and easily, but must play in time – and in tune as well. They also have to know how to dance along as they play. Apart from combining skills, the actors are expected to excel in this or that skill in particular. At one moment, during army drill, they do *pliés* and other balletic exercises with great aplomb, ballet here appropriately parodying military rigour. At another they burst out singing in perfect chorus, as when they sing the student song that gives the production its title. Their vocal strength does not fail them even when they sing from beneath the floorboards.

Elsewhere the actors show their mastery of balance, as happens when a grand piano is let down by ropes from the rafters for an orgy involving booze and drugs. A woman and a man play a musical-sexual duet on it, and pick out the dominant theme of Mozart's G Minor Symphony with their toes before the piano is lifted back up, carrying them and their euphoria up with it as it swings. The parodic glory of it is reinforced by the sudden upsurge of a full orchestra on record loudly playing Mozart's theme.

The flying piano is an exception to the rule of *Gaudeamus*, which is that space is extended from the floor downwards. In *Claustrophobia*, by contrast, space continually goes up, encompassing space for movement mid-air and up the walls. Once again, the actors are challenged to stretch their technical skills. They scale what look like the walls of a dance studio right to the top (it is, in fact, a replica of Dodin's teaching studio at the Theatre Academy). They enter and exit through open windows at stage right, and towards the end of the performance just walk through the walls – parts of which are made of paper, which they tear open to pass through, parts of plaster, through which they knock holes with builders' tools. During the course of the performance they walk, stand, or sit on the barres attached to

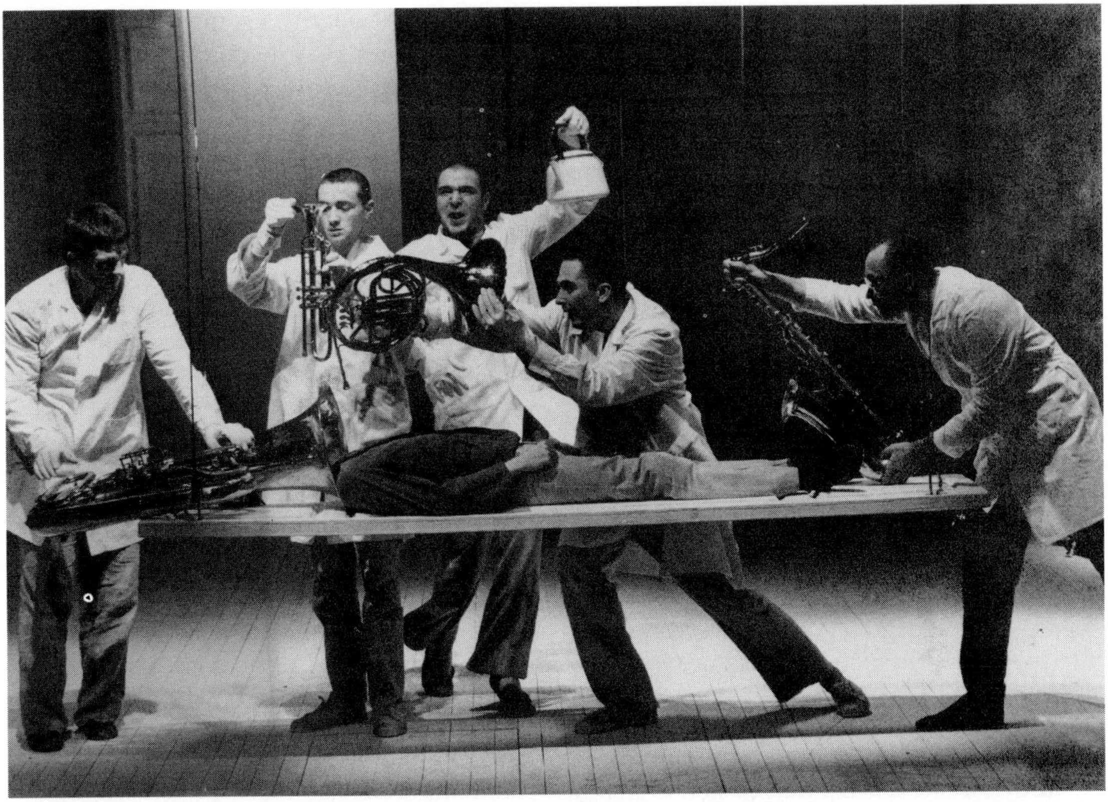

From the Maly Drama Theatre's production of *Claustrophobia*. Photos: Ken Reynolds.

the walls, or else do ballet steps on top of them. All these movements occur during dialogue or song.

Displacement – and the Fin de Siècle

These feats draw attention to themselves *as* feats – a self-reference or reflexivity which, together with the lack of narrative or causal connection in *Claustrophobia*, and its delight in fragmentation, takes the work towards a so-called postmodern theatre. Not that *Claustrophobia* is postmodern to the core. It is neither without subject-matter nor 'neutral' (two essentials of hard-rock postmodernism) because it is driven by critical perception as to what the Soviet Union has been and what Russia, after perestroika, has become.

However, instead of being confrontational (as is the case of parts of *Gaudeamus* and all of *Stars in the Morning Sky*), the production's criticism is transmuted into farce. A good example of this concerns a platform which descends from the flies and holds a prostrate body that looks like Lenin. The goose-step of soldiers in grey uniform beneath the platform indicates that the scene is Lenin's mausoleum in Moscow. What follows is a raucous, mad number in which brass instruments are played full blast, as if to awaken the dead – or used as medical instruments (drip-feeds, syringes, stethoscopes) to keep the 'patient' alive. The scene has a savage kick quite unlike its 'flying trapeze' counterpart in *Gaudeamus*.

Claustrophobia, then, is a laboratory piece with intentions that transcend its purely formal or purely theatrical experimentation. One of its themes, disjointed though it may be by the production's idiom, has to do with displacement. A group of people returning from abroad find that neither they nor the home that they had left behind are the same. They are not capable of adequately engaging with the changes that they, as well as their society, have undergone – and the tension between personal and wider social change has in large measure to do with the spatio-temporal disjunction between them, since one lot of change went on, in another time and place, without the other.

Strange though this may seem, it is precisely through this thematic nexus that *Claustrophobia* becomes a *fin de siècle* version (from the vantage point of our own *fin de siècle*, of course) of *The Cherry Orchard*. Ranyevskaya, too, has returned home to an unrecognizable Russia, and cannot deal with it any more than she can deal with changes in herself. The relationship between the two productions may be fortuitous – in that *Claustrophobia* may simply have washed over into *The Cherry Orchard*, as happens when several pieces of work are prepared simultaneously. On the other hand, the reverse may have occurred, with Dodin's sense of Chekhov infiltrating *Claustrophobia*.

Whatever the case may be, it is certain that there are thematic links between the two productions, which affect how Dodin conceives of his staging for both of them. These connections are accentuated by the similarity not of the productions' decor as such, but of what is done to it. *Claustrophobia* ends with the outright vandalizing of the room-studio inhabited by its performers. Kochergin's set for *The Cherry Orchard* is a group of tall, diptych and triptych screens in the shape of altar windows. It is progressively, if rather unobtrusively, dismantled during the last two acts of the performance until, by the end, only its skeleton remains – torn apart by unseen hands, not destroyed by the characters themselves, as is the case in *Claustrophobia*.

The set gives Ranyevskaya's house and orchard in one, the latter suggested by the branches of flowers attached to several of the panes of the 'altar' windows. Both house and orchard are elliptically sketched in by other means as well, notably through the 'corridors' created by the arrangement of the altar-screens. The actors walk in and out of these – now indicating the interior of the house, now the orchard outside it. They dance as they weave in and around them during the ball scene in the third act. Their hands are linked in a chain, and they dance on and on, evoking by their seeming inability to stop images of the dance of death.

Kochergin's construction is dark, not quite black to the eye since its panels are lit

From the Maly production of *The Cherry Orchard.* Left to right: Nikolai Lavrov as Pischik, Sergei Kurishev as Trofimov, and Angelica Nevolina as Charlotta. Photo: Ken Reynolds.

from behind by small lamps. Porai-Kochits' scenery is pristine white – the floor, barres, radiators, and all – except for the paneless windows at stage right that open on to the empty darkness behind them. Both designs are brilliant solutions to Dodin's reflections on how design-space must capture the intentions of the mise en scène – that is to say, how the visual and performance components must work together, and do so interpretively in concert for the logic and dynamics of the whole.

Ancient Tragedy Replayed

Claustrophobia ends in images of willful, violent destruction, *The Cherry Orchard* in those of crumbling ruin. The implication behind these contrasting perspectives could well be that they are two views, from two different angles, of the same phenomenon – the disintegration of an edifice, of a house. This house functions as a metaphor in both productions for Russia: consequently, its disintegration is Russia's disintegration.

Dodin's line of vision, from where he stands to survey the panorama, starts from the turn of the twentieth century with *The Cherry Orchard* and ends with *Claustrophobia* on the brink of a new millennium. As Dodin's gaze sweeps across space, time contracts in that its two ends converge on a central spot. In other words, from Dodin's site of contemplation, nothing much appears to distinguish the past from the present: the demise of Russia at the beginning of the century is replayed, albeit by different players in different circumstances, at its end. It has all the fatality of antique tragedy.

Dodin's pessimistic and even despairing outlook on Russia's history underlies all seven of the productions grouped together

315

in this overview. Yet the sense of a unity between all the collaborators involved in them – performers, of course, included – is so strong that the productions do not come across as being merely vehicles for a director's personal vision. They convey, instead, what could well and truly be called the Maly's world view. This could be put differently by saying that the complicity between Dodin and his collaborators is so fine that in the ensuing osmosis emerges a gestalt-like cohesion of artistic perception and projection.

What is projected through performance is multi-faceted and by no means uniform in tone. Some works have a deeper colouring than others. Nevertheless, despite the dark undercurrents that weave through them, the seven productions are enormously resilient and buoyant works – the resilience and the buoyancy not arising from a desire to put on a brave face in public, but springing from a surging life-force, from a life-wish that adversity cannot quell.

It is this very desire to live, no matter what the obstacles to living may be, that propels *The Cherry Orchard*. Irrespective of how Ranyevskaya's estate crumbles – visibly in the time-space of the performance – and even irrespective of the last, deeply moving moments that witness Firs dying on stage, all the actors firmly convey the life-wish that motivates their characters. Evgeny Lebedev, who plays Firs, lies down on the sofa and holds a candle to his chest – a sociocultural sign if ever there was one, in that it refers specifically to Russian Orthodox funeral rites. The candle then falls from his hands. (Lebedev is a highly venerated old actor, as old as one could imagine Firs to be, who was 'borrowed' for the role from the St Petersburg Bolshoi Drama Theatre, which achieved fame during the Soviet period under Georgy Tovstonogov.)

Each character has his/her own trajectory, which, apart from marking out its path clearly in the patterns of the whole, leaves its traces behind after the performance has come to a close. This means that, despite the formal closure provided by Firs's death, the production is remarkably open-ended.

Ranyevskaya (Tatyana Shestakova, Anfisa in *Brothers and Sisters*) is performed as a loving, radiant woman who is freed by the auction of her orchard to take on her future. Although full of uncertainties, she assumes it: it is *her* future. Gaev (Sergei Bekhterev, Verkhovensky in *The Devils*), though boyish, fastidious, and silly, is energized by his memories of his childhood, and leaves the impression, when he quits the stage, that he will manage, somehow.

Varya (a nuanced, funny-obsessive performance from Natalya Akimova, Lizka in *Brothers and Sisters*) is played as a woman driven by her own unfulfilled potential and, although all nerves rather than energy, she will keep on keeping on. Charlotta (Angelica Nevolina, prostitute Maria in *Stars in the Morning Sky*), swirling in on the shoulders of a man, her long skirts covering him, and accompanied by a poodle, does delightful magical tricks with handkerchiefs, gherkins, and Russian-doll skirts. She keenly feels her orphaned state, as her oddities and whimsical jokes show, but will doggedly continue to resist her own fragility.

Pishchik (Nikolai Lavrov, Ivan in *Brothers and Sisters*), who is played in a lively and engaging manner, though he sticks like a leech, is besotted by Ranyevskaya, but has a head cool enough to save himself from bankruptcy. In the same stroke, he secures his daughter's future. Ranyevskaya was able to do neither. She hopelessly fails Varya, who is not just a hanger-on but her adopted daughter – a failure lucidly brought out by the production without condemning her, though not quite condoning her either.

Lopakhin (Igor Ivanov, Egorsha in *The House*) is an extremely ambiguous figure, sure that the time for balls and orchards has passed. He partly recalls crass, wheeler-dealer New Russians, as this breed emerged after perestroika, and partly the 'respectable', smart businessmen who also emerged from the New Russia. He will amass a fortune, and yet Ranyevskaya will always remain his icon, driving him on to ransack what in his heart of hearts he desires to possess purely and not with money, dirty or clean. (I have given examples of alternate roles for the actors cited here and previously in order to suggest just how wide their range is.)

This synopsis is far from complete, since it not only passes by other roles in silence, but also does not draw in the cruel, hard lines of Chekhov's universe, of which the Maly is fully aware. Nor does it indicate adequately that every role, however it is traditionally conceived as minor, is interpreted as a major one. Firs is a case in point. Lebedev magisterially turns him into an exemplar of quirky yet compulsive devotion whose life blood is memory: but he is in fact everybody's memory, even Russia's collective memory, which appears to have faded out of everybody's sight. The country's future is just as nebulous for sheer neglect.

The Quality of Being Unfinished

The Maly's *Cherry Orchard* is guided by the idea that forgetting and forgetfulness efface all too quickly the relations that people build between them and the life together that they build out of them. With this in mind, it strives to hold on to the warmth and affection that its protagonists, actors as much as characters, have for each other. And what it leaves behind is a feeling of apprehension, a gnawing fear that such warmth is terribly vulnerable: like Firs's candle, it is just as likely to slip out of everybody's hands. Firs's time comes to a natural end. Time for the rest of them, the production seems to infer, may well have run out before their time is up.

There appears to be no natural end possible to this tonally fluctuating, curiously unsettled *Cherry Orchard*. The unresolved air hanging around the production stays on, longer than the lights after Firs dies. Only time will tell, as the Maly refines and redefines its *Cherry Orchard* in the cumulative manner peculiar to it, whether its general air of uncertainty will endure; whether this indecisiveness endures for reasons to do with intention and interpretation, say, with Dodin's anxiety not to trivialize Chekhov or make him too obviously relevant to today; whether, when, and if such inner conflicts as to interpretation are set to rest, the work will remain feeling unfinished – not only open-ended, which it already is, and which is another characteristic altogether, but also *unfinished*.

If the quality of being unfinished survives, then it will have established itself as a compositional element integral, along with others, to the production's overall conception. In which case, it will probably have consolidated the tragic strain underlying the production as it is now performed, especially as its latent tragedy has already taken hold more firmly since the work was premiered in 1994. If the Maly's working methods of time-flow, gestation, and accumulation fully absorb this particular stream, its *Cherry Orchard* will have opened out, in the process, a much deeper tragic vein in Chekhov than Chekhov would ever have wished to acknowledge.

The fact of Chekhov's writing *The Cherry Orchard* virtually on his death-bed does not alone explain the play's dark pull. For it *does* have a tragic dimension which Chekhov's legendary elusiveness not only as a writer but also as a human being has successfully masked. As is well known, Stanislavsky perceived it, much to Chekhov's annoyance, judging by his famous critical remarks on the director's approach. Dodin and the Maly have probed behind this elusiveness. If the tragic Chekhov hidden in Chekhov surfaces unequivocally from their production – and, more still, resurfaces again in the anticipated Chekhov cycle – then we may well discover that we live in far more tragic times than any of us is able yet to recognize, let alone understand.

John Tulloch, Tom Burvill, and Andrew Hood

Reinhabiting 'The Cherry Orchard': Class and History in Performing Chekhov

Chekhov's *The Cherry Orchard* is clearly 'about' the end of one social order – about time changing and time static. Yet different interpretive communities – academics in journal articles and students in their classrooms, newspaper reviewers, theatre writers like Trevor Griffiths and David Mamet, and theatre directors like Adrian Noble and Richard Eyre – 'read' Chekhov's representation of history and class change in different ways. The authors of this study have been exploring these different reading formations in a three-year project funded by the Australian Research Council, 'Chekhov: in Criticism, Performance, and Reading'. Here – grounding their work in industry 'readings' via production study and interviews – they focus on production and performance of *The Cherry Orchard*, contrasting the Richard Eyre/Trevor Griffiths production of 1977 (reproduced in 1981 for BBC TV) with Adrian Noble's production at the Swan Theatre, Stratford, in 1995. In particular, they discuss the writing, directing, acting, and staging of Chekhov's 'modernity' in these productions, suggesting that whereas Noble referenced and yet simultaneously occluded class in his rehearsal style and staging, Griffiths and Eyre worked for a production which not only embodied the intra-class mobility of the Thatcher era in 1981, but also the 'then' of Chekhov's own particular engagement with modernity and environment. John Tulloch, Professor of Cultural Studies at Charles Sturt University, New South Wales, is author of *Chekhov: a Structuralist Study*. Tom Burvill is Associate Professor of Drama and Cultural Studies at Macquarie University, Sydney, where Andrew Hood is a PhD student working on reception cultures.

I think the issue of class is fantastically important . . . that the people who owned most of the land in Chekhov's plays did not live there. Now that's an important *fact*, a materialist fact which leads to relationships that are on the one hand fantastically strong and passionate, because there's an 'over there' immediately, there's a Moscow . . . and on the other hand there's a fury because they're . . . exploited places. *Adrian Noble*[1]

The Cherry Orchard has *always* seemed to me to be dealing not only with the subjective pain of property-loss but also more importantly with its objective *necessity*. *Trevor Griffiths*[2]

I rather like productions where there's a link between Lopakhin and Trofimov . . . and . . . he admires his beautiful artist's hands. They can't cope with women either of them, they prefer each other. I don't mind a slight gay interpretation, just a very slight touch. But a very strong sociological rising forces/decaying forces interpretation I think is a betrayal. *Donald Rayfield*[3]

WHEN WE RECENTLY surveyed all English-speaking academic criticism of Chekhov published in books and in refereed articles between 1980 and 1995, it become clear that Donald Rayfield's concern, above, about the 'betrayal' of 'strong sociological' or 'class' readings of *The Cherry Orchard* is common among current Chekhov scholars.[4] The same research project, however, indicates that this is not the same in other interpretive communities. 'Rising forces/decaying forces' interpretations of *The Cherry Orchard* are standard in newspaper reviewing; and issues of class and social change can also exercise leading British theatre practitioners, as we see from Adrian Noble's and Trevor Griffiths's comments above.

There are, of course, plenty of theatre people who would agree with Rayfield. David Mamet specifically rejects the notion that *The Cherry Orchard* is cherished because 'it is about the struggle between the Old Values of the Russian Aristocracy and their loosening grasp on power'.[5] For Mamet the 'social states of its characters . . . separate us from the play.' Rather, the 'enduring draw' of *The Cherry Orchard* is that 'we subconsciously perceive and enjoy the reiterated action of this reiterated scene: two people at odds – each trying to fulfil his or her frustrated sexuality'.

Yet when Mamet's adaptation of *The Cherry Orchard* is used on the stage – as with the New Theatre's late-1996 production in Sydney – issues of social order and social change can and do re-emerge. Comparing the relevance of Chekhov's Russia with the significant social change at the end of the Labour years in power in Australia, director Mary-Anne Gifford disagreed with Mamet in her programme notes:

I don't agree that the play is only about a lot of couples wanting to get it off with each other. . . . I think it's about the repression of passion of all kinds (not only sexual). . . . Repression . . . implies a kind of passivity in the face of life. . . . Love, sex, passion, freedom, change, risk.[6]

Our initial point is that the critique of 'rising forces/decaying forces' in *The Cherry Orchard* is very much stronger and more consensual in academia than on the pages and stages of the theatre industry. What interests us, though, is neither Griffiths's and Noble's implicit rejection of Rayfield's charge of vulgar sociological reductionism, nor Gifford's rejection of Mamet's 'frustrated sexuality' reading, but rather the ways in which class, 'freedom, change, risk', and history are worked through in these different theatre practices.

In this article we will examine the construction of class and history in Chekhov on the stage, comparing two British productions of *The Cherry Orchard* with the intention of relating the material practices of writers, directors, and actors to performance readings of Chekhov.[7] In doing this, we will focus in particular (as does Rayfield) on the relationship of the social 'change agents', Lopakhin and Trofimov. In the case of these two productions of *The Cherry Orchard* – the Eyre/Griffiths production, seen at Nottingham in 1977 and on BBC Television in 1981, and Adrian Noble's, seen at Stratford in 1995 and in London the following year – class and history were staged and performed in complexly different ways. The performance that Griffiths/Eyre were looking for in Lopakhin can be traced through their relationship with the two actors who played the part in their productions of *The Cherry Orchard*. Trevor Griffiths emphasized significant differences between Dave Hill's 1977 performance of Lopakhin at Nottingham Playhouse and Bill Patterson's in the 1981 television production.

Griffiths, Eyre, and Performing Lopakhin

Griffiths evaluated these differences on the one hand according to the particular balance of turn-of-the-century 'organic' environmental and merchant qualities that he believed he had rediscovered in Chekhov, and on the other according to the specific decade in which each production was performed. Performances of Chekhov had for Griffiths necessarily to change according to their time and space (theatre, television, satellite, etc) co-ordinates. But in addition, there must be Chekhov's historical Lopakhin, whom Griffiths felt he was rediscovering:

Lopakhin begins to talk about the poppy field in bloom. Now, there's two things going on here. He talks about the poppy field and he talks about how much it's worth. And in my version of that play both things have got to be very strong: both the natural, organic dimension of a poppy field, and the accountancy. At Nottingham, Dave Hill got that on the stage, though he leaned towards the natural dimension of the poppy field. Bill never got anywhere near that. He always had a calculator in his pocket. He was clicking up what it was worth.[8]

Since Griffiths's interpretation of Lopakhin was a significant presence at both rehearsals, the actors' own differences in inflecting the writer's concepts and politics become interesting.

Patterson told us that his emphasis in performing Lopakhin was the context of 1980s intra-Tory mobility:

We did it very much of the time: early 1980s . . . when the . . . nouveau riche were beginning to take over. . . . The Thatcher period, where you had the entrepreneurial class rising above the landed aristocracy, the old Tory class. That had very strong relevance in this country . . . and we talked a lot about it in rehearsal. . . . I think Lopakhin probably made more sense at that time than he'd done for a couple of decades.[9]

This 1980s 'strong relevance' led Patterson to emphasize his 'poppy field' lines in the fourth act:

In the same way as a farmer looks at rape seed oil that we get in Britain today, these . . . yellow fields we have just now, which are all part of the EEC money that's come in to grow this stuff . . . they're dazzling and they pop up everywhere. And you can see more money being poured into them.

As Stanton B. Garner emphasizes, though, Griffiths's own construction of 'relevance' goes beyond any one specific historical moment, such as Patterson's 'the Thatcher period'. It inheres in 'forms of dialogue between different historical moments' and therefore in playing 'the balance between relevance and difference'.[10] Griffiths wanted Lopakhin to contain a multiple historical subjectivity; and the 1904 Lopakhin was to be more than an upwardly mobile nouveau-Tory. Thus Griffiths became unhappy with Patterson's 'poppy field' interaction with Trofimov in Act IV, especially since these lines are spoken in response to Trofimov's 'You've an artist's hands', which, as Rayfield notes, betrays an unspoken closeness between them.

For Griffiths, *The Cherry Orchard* needed to play *between* the 1980s neo-conservative Lopakhin (which Patterson made of him) and the 1904 'builder' of beauty that director Richard Eyre also emphasized:

It's so often you see the audience being invited to take the side of Gayev and Ranevskaya, and think 'the vulgarity of it – Lopakhin's ruining this beautiful cherry orchard'. What's so wonderful about the play is all its complexities. Because the cherry orchard is beautiful. It is a magnificent work of nature – but of course a work of nature that has been appropriated and is owned by people who regard nature as their property. And there is this man who is taking over this piece of property, but at least he is using it to give happiness to a lot more people. They may be more of the bourgeoisie, but actually it's giving happiness – it's spreading it around a bit.[11]

Bill Patterson, however, played the 'poppy field lines' with his back to camera, where his desultory shrug (immediately between 'That's something to behold, I can tell you, a poppy field in bloom' and 'Anyway, I made 40,000') is what conveys his mood. On television in particular, a conventional shot of Lopakhin's 'two eyes' over the poppy field lines could have conveyed for an instant a very different, much more idealistic vision. But, as Patterson said:

I played it with a sense of . . . him getting embarrassed . . . 'that's something to behold I can tell you, the poppy field in bloom'. And it was as though it was a sign of weakness because maybe the cherry orchard would have been nice as well but – anyway . . . I made the forty thousand and you're welcome to some of it. . . . The beauty is the poppies he planted, which are making money. . . . Poppy seeds or opium or anything could have come from these. . . . So it would be a cash crop to him of course, rather than a thing of beauty.

Dave Hill, performing the part in 1977, came closer than Patterson to adopting the symptomatic Griffiths signature of playing 'the balance between relevance and difference'. On the one hand he related Lopakhin to both the brutalizing experiences of turn-of-the-century Russia and to his own recent class experience:

I read Gorky's *My Childhood* and we based a lot of . . . the back history of Lopakhin, on that. . . . Gorky, like Lopakhin, did get beaten. We used that at the Russian end, and, because I like my acting to relate directly into the English situation, I used also the fact that I was brought up . . . in an English working-class northern family, so we based him around that sort of structure of moving through the class system.

This was a differently positioned class mobility from Patterson's Thatcherite reference, and moreover it replicated Griffiths's own history. Trevor Griffiths was also upwardly mobile from a northern working-class family; and for Richard Eyre this was significant in his choice of Griffiths as collaborator on *The Cherry Orchard*:

You cast actors to the part and you cast writers to the play, and it just seemed entirely to correspond to Trevor's strengths. . . . There's a lot of Lopakhin in Trevor. . . . There's an element in him that finds Lopakhin very attractive . . . you know, working-class background guy who's worked very, very hard to emerge from his class background. . . . There's a sense in which his life is a sort of triumph of 'I've bought the cherry orchard'.

What is interesting here is the way in which concepts of the *contemporaneity* of class were active in quite different ways in the two productions. For Griffiths and Hill there was a sense of contestation between their own class trajectory and the conservative politics of their own time, in clear comparison with Patterson's replication of 1980s Tory intra-class struggle. But in addition neither Hill nor Griffiths tried to construct Lopakhin only in terms of contemporary class experience. There was also the particularity of Lopakhin's own time and place: there were Chekhov's own comments on Lopakhin being the central character of the play, and his emphasis on Lopakhin as artist as well as merchant.

The Cambridge academic Peter Holland emphasized that historical particularity of Lopakhin (and Chekhov) very clearly when he interviewed Adrian Noble on the stage of the Swan Theatre in January 1996:

I've always thought that one of the big problems for English audiences in watching Chekhov is that we know exactly what should happen to the cherry orchard. It should be given to the National Trust! . . . That's an English sensibility of what happens to a great estate. And when we hear Lopakhin in the play talking about dividing it up for lots for summer cottages, it always sounds a bit odd to us and not really what you're supposed to do. . . . But Chekhov surely saw that as a very *positive* thing. He had his little dacha in the country, and many Russians do. We need that consciousness of how different this world is – its values are different – that even the middle class is not the same middle class.

Dave Hill reached for this particularity of the 'artistic' Lopakhin in a slightly different but related way. Shortly before playing Lopakhin, Dave Hill had been to Eastern Europe and seen their 'very serious dream' of 'getting away and being at one with yourself' by growing things in small country dachas. As a result he felt that he understood better Lopakhin's plan of subdividing the cherry orchard estate:

Those [poppy field] lines were a wonderful combination of beauty, almost like it was a painting but also the feeling of getting your hands dirty at the same time, which I think is some sort of key to unlocking the man – that he has the ability actually to get down and dig . . . and plant the field himself. . . . The beauty of what you gain from life is enhanced by the fact that that's what you've done; and the fact that you are making money from it is not incidental. . . . It's all right to make money because you are somebody who is going to use it well. . . . Money as a form of energy has got to be kept moving round.

It was that sense of the expansiveness of class mobility – as a 'form of energy that has to be kept moving round', so that the ownership of property resides in people who 'actually get down and dig' – that identified Hill's performance with Richard Eyre's sense of using property 'to give happiness to a lot more people'.

Whereas Patterson positioned his contemporary Lopakhin in terms of the new Thatcherite national agenda, Hill, playing the part in what he called the 'dog days' of the ever more conservative Labour government, found no direct contemporary political reference for Lopakhin's expansive 'form of energy'. Instead he found his Lopakhin through his trip to Eastern Europe, mediated via his father's class memory:

A patriarchal figure of Victorian mill owner standards. . . . Somebody like Alexander Salt, a person who builds a model village for his workers, but would still want to live in the big house. . . . He had that similarity with a lot of Victorian mill owners. My father was brought up in the cotton trade and there was that . . . dream that there would be a decent life for everybody.

Hill was constructing his part, in other words, in a play between the 'then' and the 'now': of *both* his own and the Gorky intertext's class memory; and of *both* Chekhov's Russian and the contemporary Eastern European 'serious dream' of land ownership. This was more satisfying for Trevor Griffiths because it was closer to his own view of producing history.[12] In Griffiths's words:

The danger in writing a history play is that people think it is about then. The lie in writing one is to pretend that it is always and only about now. Somewhere in between the lie and the danger is a truth that you can uncover.[13]

That 'truth you can uncover' is not, of course, for Griffiths or Hill based on an 'originary' artistic consciousness. For both, it is very clear that parts are constructed dialogically (in Bakhtin's sense) in negotiation between different historical times, narratives, memories, and intertexts. For Hill this included Gorky, Griffiths, his father, his recent experience in Eastern Europe, and so on. For Griffiths there was also a significant intertextual play between Chekhov's texts and Raymond Williams's reading of them – and this relationship between Griffiths and Williams was itself embedded in issues of history and class relating to the formation of the New Left in the 1950s.[14]

Reading Formation: Williams and Griffiths

It is clear from both Griffiths's statements and his work that Raymond Williams has been a significant reading formation for him.[15] Griffiths, however, also *transforms* Williams's Chekhov text (primarily as in *Drama from Ibsen to Brecht*) by constructing a sub-textual narrative in Act II of *The Cherry Orchard*,[16] where he connects the alienated characters that Williams foregrounds with what he calls the 'incredible disjuncture' of the vagrant – this in itself motivating Trofimov's later line (in Griffiths's version), 'In your orchard there are people hanging.'

Griffiths's text reads the beginning of Act II non-naturalistically, where a taped voice-over marks an immediate contrast with the heightened naturalism of Act I. The actors (whom Griffiths wants stretched across the stage at the opening of Act II 'as on a telephone wire' and 'staring out at the audience') are intended to convey 'a field of meaning . . . a mesh, a mosaic . . . rather than a line of meanings, a univalence'.[17] For Griffiths, this particular 'polyphonic' staging works both as a modernist device and to emphasize the characters' aspirations to modernity (as with Charlotta, Yepihodov, Yasha, and Dunyasha). Charlotta, for instance, is deprived of passport, citizenship, national identity –

a character edging towards Kafka, edging towards statelessness, edging towards . . . 'Who am I? How can I define an identity, a self identity, without a state, without values, without history?'[18]

Griffiths's narrative 'sub-text' for Act II thus energizes this loss of citizenship and identity via his use of Trofimov and Lopakhin. In Griffiths's view, these 'outsiders' are the only characters with a vision of a future which can work on the servant and under-class group's 'unachievable, almost inarticulate desires for things that are better, and yearning to know why they aren't'.

Lopakhin and Trofimov, as the agents of change, contextualize in different ways for Griffiths the 'breaking string' of Act II, which, far from being Williams's 'inert symbol', is rather a signifier of discontinuity with the past – of rupture, dislocation, a 'cable groaning under stress'. Here Chekhov, in Griffiths's 'rediscovery', is working 'below the text, rather than arching above it in monumental, statuesque symbolism. There's so much that is alive and pulsing below the line that it's almost unplayable.'

In particular, it is the energy of the underclass that is 'pulsing below the line'. Thus there is 'a direct relationship between the rupture notion [of the cable groaning under stress] and the shift to the stranger. The stranger is what is ushered in by the rupturing of present and past over which . . . the characters on the stage . . . have no control'.

Griffiths's reading of Chekhov's modernity is indicated by his 'sub-textual narrative'– linking the breaking cable, Firs's comment about 'The Freedom', Trofimov's speech to Anya about people hanging from the cherry trees, and the appearance of the vagrant (dressed in Griffiths's text in a First World War greatcoat):

It seems to me that the word 'freedom' has now been unleashed in this text, and it resonates throughout the play. . . . The heart of the scene for me is the arrival of the stranger. . . . Nobody from that underclass has ever appeared . . . in Chekhov's kind of drama. . . . Released by the French Revolution a hundred years previously and still wandering, still looking for social justice, equality, fraternity. And, clearly, failing to find it here. But . . . by presenting that person with such extraordinary menace . . . [Chekhov] metamorphizes . . . the property loss that is facing them as a problem . . . and destabilizes any notion the audience might have had of a settled world, their settled world. . . . I think this moment really says there is a great unavoidable black hole underneath our world, and very soon we will disappear into it and become a pellet of energy for a new world.[19]

Symptomatically working between the text 'then' and the audience 'now', Griffiths clearly still believes in class change, and in theatre's powerful capacity for cultural intervention. The narrative conjuncture of the stranger with Trofimov's words to Anya permits Chekhov's peasants – who (as Griffiths emphasizes) populate his more 'sociological' stories but, for reasons of stage convention and market ideology, are absent from his plays – to 'explode on to the stage'.

In contrast, Adrian Noble's *The Cherry Orchard* constructs modernity very differently; and here it is the 'light and love' of Ranevskaya's memories, not the peasants, that explode onto the stage.

Class and History in Noble's Production

Adrian Noble, as we have seen, also emphasizes the centrality of class to *The Cherry Orchard*. But, crucially, Noble positions these 'two great forces' in terms of an inability to grow up within his contained 'house' of *The Cherry Orchard*:

The play in a way is about the house. It creates a microcosm of the world, and there are folk *representing* all the different social strata of society and all the different pressures that are struggling inside society – it's all inside this house, so it is a finite world that contains all this cocktail of elements. And in a way the most fraught moment of the play is the dispersal, when they go; and that's the vacuum, that's the dispersal that leads to the chaos that began in Russia within twelve months of him writing the play. . . . There's this curious 'We cling to the past': that's Liuba's and Gayev's great sin,

they cannot let go, they cling, they hang on to the wreckage, and they will not take responsibility . . . will not face up to reality. They *dance* while the house is being sold. . . . And that is to do with an inability to grow up.

Adrian Noble's focus on 'the house' and an 'inability to grow up' led this production to a very different embodiment of class and history from the Eyre and Griffiths *Cherry Orchard*. Eyre and Griffiths foregrounded class and modernity, especially through the external setting of Act II – for Griffiths the most Brechtian act, which he felt was achieved more convincingly via the two-dimensional, minimalist staging at Nottingham than in the more naturalistic BBC Television version.

However, even in the television production Eyre emphasized a 'class/ownership' history via the staging. He set up his gentry-on-the-bench scene for Act II by drawing intertextually on John Berger's reading (in his *Ways of Seeing* television series) of Sir Kenneth Clark's interpretation of the 'Mr. and Mrs. Andrews' of Gainsborough. Commenting on the relevance of the repeat TV showing of Berger's series to this setting, Eyre said 'the whole idea of landscape as property was very much in my mind'.

Through the use of Scottish accents for the servant/serf class in the BBC Television version, the Eyre/Griffiths production also emphasized coloniality. In contrast Noble, despite his overt statements about class and coloniality in interview,[20] displaced them both via deploying the Swan Theatre as 'the house', the use of Stanislavskian rehearsal methods appealing to childhood memory, and in the infantilized construction of historical change.

Adrian Noble's production quite overtly distanced itself from Trevor Griffiths's translation and reading of the play. To choose his translation, Noble 'took half a dozen passages – the same passages – from six or seven translations' and had his PA read them to him:

Peter Gill won six out of seven times. . . . It was a very uncluttered translation. I immediately knew Trevor Griffiths's translation, *immediately*, like within two words, because it was, you know, 'Get off my shoulder Trevor, stop *leaning* on me'.

Noble's preference for Gill's 'uncluttered' version over a political interpretation which he perceived as 'leaning on' him worked through to the situating and staging of the play at the Swan Theatre – in what Noble called 'one of the most site-specific productions I think I've ever done.' Adrian Noble was pleased when Peter Holland, interviewing him on the stage of the Swan Theatre, said:

I've never seen a production of Chekhov that made me so aware that I am in a theatre, in which the theatre becomes the house. . . . The Swan seems to lend itself perfectly to a space in which we are all living in the same house.

Noble responded:

I think it's fantastic you say that. That was one of the absolutely central reasons that we wanted to do the play. Because I think what this theatre does wonderfully is, it enables the inner architecture, the skeleton of the play to reveal itself. It tends to resist . . . naturalism and realism.

Foregrounding 'the House'

In other words, whereas the reading formation of the New Left (an academic/political, dialogic, and theorized relationship between Trevor Griffiths and Raymond Williams) underpinned Griffiths's 'rediscovery' of class and history in Chekhov, for Noble it was the spatial and economic relationship with 'the house' – the Swan, which formed part of his empire as Artistic Director of the RSC – that was an 'absolutely central reason' for doing the play.

In his interview with Holland, Noble was clear about the profit potential of playing Chekhov at the Swan (and the RSC marketing officer confirmed this). Noble was also conscious of the Swan's potential to resist naturalism – though in a very different way from Griffiths's 'Brechtian' Act II:

The reason I wanted it here is that I didn't want a set. . . . We were very keen not to create rooms, not just because of the nature of this theatre but also because it seemed to me that there is a way to the heart of Chekhov that isn't the realistic or naturalistic way in. . . . It's very abstract, actually, what we eventually came up with, and indeed the way it's played.[21]

In the Swan Theatre one is more aware of the audience than in any other theatre I know. . . . The actor's presence seems to be in perfect balance with that of the audience. . . . The space humanizes the epic; makes public the private; and enables a secret grief or joy to be shared honestly.[22]

Marketing officer Sian Sterling supported this interpretation, in noting Chekhov's box-office popularity at the Swan:

Chekhov has always gone down well in the Swan Theatre. People just adore the atmosphere of the Swan, sitting there and watching Chekhov is an extremely pleasurable experience. The sympathetic nature of the theatre itself endears people to want to watch that type of play, that intimate play about a family situation.[23]

Not surprisingly, then, Noble was resistant to Peter Holland's suggestion in interview that Lopakhin is at the centre of Chekhov's play. For Noble:

The play . . . is about the house. . . . For me the centre of the play is the house and the emblem that the house develops into during the course of the evening.

This dramaturgical relationship between the 'house' and making public 'the private . . . secret grief' had as significant an effect on performing history and modernity in this text as did (in its very different way) Trevor Griffiths's narrative sub-text. Indeed, Noble constructs his own narrative via the staging, especially of Acts I and III, compared with which Williams's and Eyre/Griffiths's important Act II has 'nothing there':

I think there's a great explosion of life in Act I. . . . An energy comes in. . . . And then [in Act II] it takes us outside, and there's nothing there. And then [in Act III] we have this night-time scene back inside, with very few things, very simply, this dance of death, this ball that's happening while everything's sold off. . . . And then finally [in Act IV] the trunks, it's what you take away, its your baggage, its your past . . . packing up.

The particular emphasis that Adrian Noble gave to 'the house' in rehearsal is evident from actor Peter Copley's contrast of two different rehearsal processes he had been through playing Firs in *The Cherry Orchard*. At the Bristol Old Vic, director Paul Unwin had underpinned Griffiths's adaptation with actors' 'research tasks' which looked into the economic and class effects of the emancipation of the serfs. For Unwin, Copley had thus researched the poverty of the peasants as they became indebted to banks following the distribution of land:

They only bought little strips, which was very uneconomical, like medieval times. . . . So we did a lot of that serious research and we had . . . almost to read a paper on it.

In contrast, 'we didn't have any of that with Adrian'. In rehearsal, there was no real 'plotting, placing, and so on', and little research:

There wasn't anything on stage except for this pile of furniture and one bench. So we cleared everything off. You were not helped by anything except your own intention and determination.

Performance as Memory

So whereas Unwin supported Griffiths's search for a 'specific historicity' in rehearsal, Noble's emphasis (both physically and conceptually) was on the Swan's 'uncluttering', so that (as Copley put it) 'we cleared everything off' and actors were 'loose on stage'.

Noble emphasized to Holland that his production ignored 'the anthropological way in to drama' (as in 'first find your peasant') for an approach through actors' experiences:

The British acting tradition . . . has absorbed . . . Stanislavsky and . . . empathy, finding that in yourself that could inhabit the character, so the character became part of you, and you became part of the character. . . . So, quite contrary to my own style, we actually did quite a lot of improvisatory work . . . investigating . . . our childhoods. . . . Most of the actors had very strong sense memories of their childhoods.

This relationship between actor, history, and character in rehearsal via childhood emotions and memories had, as Kate Duchêne (Varya) explained, special relevance to the Swan Theatre as 'house':

Adrian was basically Stanislavskian in his approach. . . . He concentrated a lot on the house, and of course he loves the Swan Theatre, so for him it almost is like a house. He concentrated a lot on making the house in our minds and our imaginations. We had to do exercises, like he put two chairs in a corner and he said, 'Just walk around as your character – these two chairs are a doorway, when you feel like it just come into a room you loved as a child.' We did that and then we talked about what our rooms were, so he began to build up a picture of the house, and also a background to your character as you saw them. And then 'come into a room that you hated as a child'. . . . So slowly you got a picture of everybody's lives and of the house.

These improvised memories called up a personalized and 'property-owning' response from some of the actors quite unlike the more class-conceptualized contemporary/ historical preparations of Bill Patterson and Dave Hill. Alec McCowen (Gayev) typically related the house to particular memories during Noble's rehearsal exercises:

[The exercises] stirred memories for me because emotionally one has to love the home and the cherry orchard. So it stirred memories for me of my own childhood home and growing up and when we left it. Also I have substitute homes to think of. I have had for the last twenty-five years a home by the seaside looking over the Channel, and I thought, 'My God if I had to give that up how would I feel?' . . . So yes, those exercises that we did made me feel geographically, made me think of homes and rooms and childhood. . . . To me the play is really about my childhood which was in the 1930s and 1940s and thinking about the values of that time when we had a live-in maid. . . . Life is so different now. . . . So there is a huge, huge nostalgic element for me.

These 'childhood' rehearsal exercises had already occurred

by the point that Peter Copley was speaking of, where the rehearsing actors were 'just loose on the stage . . . not helped by anything except your own intention'. Noble's 'uncluttering' of stage and performance could never be embedded in some zero degree of intention, history, and professional value. It was, in fact, embedded in Noble's house/rooms/childhood inflection of a

Stanislavskian method. Moreover, because every actor's childhood memory was a very different one, the particular sense of history brought to this play was significantly fragmented, united only by 'the house'.

Staging History

Both Griffiths's 'rediscovery' of Chekhov's peasants and Noble's 'reinhabiting' of Chekhov's house were based on a sense of abstraction beyond naturalism, and both constructed (and performed) modernity. But Griffiths wanted his 'modernist' Act II to breach the naturalistic surface of appearances of the other acts. Similarly, his underclass 'explosion' in the sub-text was intended to breach the 'insider' world of the cherry orchard people.

In contrast, Noble's focus on the 'uncluttered' (in theatre as in translation) and on personal childhood memory led to a fragmenting across personal histories which the director countered by staging a 'house' history of his own. Act I opened with the lifting of a gauze box on a virtually setless stage, accompanied by the sound of a train. For Noble:

Chekhov had this great skill to offer to an audience – just a few objects or just a few effects that, like a drip in water, will emanate out, will reverberate through the play. So the trains were, to me, terribly important, the thing of arriving, travelling – 'Oh, the old master used to go by coach, now they travel by train.' They arrive back on the train, and they leave on the train. Most of the great and usually tragic moments in twentieth-century European history involve trains.

Like Griffiths/Eyre, then, Noble emphasized modernity. His assistant director, Andrew Cooper, elaborated on this:

Adrian decided that it was very interesting to think of the train as the twentieth-century conveyor of events. The First and Second World Wars were transmitted around Europe by train. It's the technological revolution which has taken with it everything at various times.

For Trevor Griffiths modernity was signified by the agency of the vagrant who wanders in search of freedom from the 1790s to the days of Thatcher. For Noble modernity was conveyed by the 'tragic' determinacy of a technology which 'takes everything with it at various times'.

Not coincidentally, the master image that Noble suggested for the frenetic ball scene of Act III was another technologically 'tragic moment in twentieth-century European history' – the sinking of the Titanic. Cooper commented:

Adrian articulated Act III repeatedly with the image of the Titanic going down and the dance band on the Titanic playing as the ship was holed and began to sink. . . . We were working for the freneticism of the music, with the idea of it being the last dance of the Titanic, with the contrast between the party happening and the tension mounting about everything.

Here Noble's infantilizing of characters who *dance* while the house is being sold' is being embedded in a deterministic history of modernity. Movement designer Sue Lefton also spoke of Noble's use of the analogy of a sinking ship for her spectacularly choreographed dance in Act III:

The world is about to change. . . . Everything is about to disintegrate. . . . We felt that it wasn't just a dance . . . but it needed to . . . become manic. . . . We felt that the stage itself should appear to tip and tip and tip. . . . Adrian said it's like a ship . . . at sea – tipping and everyone slipping down one side, and then tipping and everyone slipping down the other way. . . . And therefore we came up with a polka which is a sort of wild dance, even though Chekhov wanted a waltz. . . . I think we achieved the kind of energy of building and building and losing your mind.

Reviewers picked up this interpretation:

Noble is . . . totally aware that the music and the dancing are part of the play's scaffolding. He uses both to drive the scene along at what seems like breakneck speed: there is a feeling of madness and inevitability – and, of course, of loss, when the music stops.[24]

Thus in Noble's production we do indeed find a 'rising/decaying forces sociological reductionism', in that the agency of those seeking citizenship (as in Griffiths/Eyre) is replaced by the mute inevitability of modernity. Like the gilded rich of the Titanic,

Liuba and Gayev *must* go down as the band plays on. The play between class, history, and modernity here is less between 'now' and 'then', as in Griffiths/Eyre, than between the 'reinhabiting' light and energy of old class memory and the (sometimes tragic) 'inevitability' of social change. In the end, the 'uncluttering' of text and stage becomes an alibi for this fated memory. As Noble himself put it:

We created a room that had nothing apart from a pile of things. . . . This way of doing it enabled us, we felt, to inhabit Act I better, because I think there's a great explosion of life in Act II. . . . The house is reinhabited with light, the spirit that Liuba . . . has and brings in to the house, and takes it over. And things are revealed. An energy comes in.

Griffiths and Noble both speak of 'energy'. Griffiths claims to 'rediscover' the peasants of Chekhov's stories and explode them onto the stage via his Act II sub-text. Noble 'reinhabits' the Swan/house with an 'explosion' of gentry memory, light, and spirit, conveyed by acting, lighting, sound, and choreography.

So, symptomatically, the most extravagant lighting shift of the production was at this moment of Liuba's return. Fragments of 'modernity' (the train sound) introduce this 'explosion of life' represented by Ranevskaya, and it is she who 'reveals' and 'reinhabits' the house. But (like the Titanic metaphor of Act III) in Noble's production symbols of modernity tend to proclaim the inevitable failure of that light and energy – and predict the return of the enclosing gauze box at the end of Act IV.

The shift from Enlightenment space to minimalist place, and from Griffiths's 'vagrant' history to the very different particularity of the Swan Theatre, embodied a different positioning of 'class' and history in Noble's production. Despite his comment to Holland about class exploitation in Russia, Noble's central discursive move in explaining his comic and tragic *Cherry Orchard* people is in fact essentialist, and determined by recurring and generational infantilist or 'childhood' tendencies across a range of characters. Thus the 'dance of death' is taken out of Griffiths's 'objective [but agentive] comedy' of class history, and is situated instead (via a legitimating reference to Lenin) in the cycle of generations:

They hang on to the wreckage and they will not take responsibility. . . . They just will not face up to reality. They dance while the house is being sold, they won't look at it. And that is to do with an inability to grow up. . . . And the children they breed . . . then can't do that either. Anya has fantasies, as does Trofimov. His form of politics is unreal – there's actually a pamphlet that Lenin wrote called 'Left-wing Communism – an Infantile Disorder' . . . and you could say that's what Trofimov falls into . . . an infantile disorder.

Rather than Griffiths's play between 'then' and 'now', Adrian Noble's understanding of history and class in *The Cherry Orchard* is of a cross-class 'then' of infantile disorder, while the 'now' is worked through individual actors' experiences – not in Dave Hill's or Bill Patterson's overt 'class mobility', but via a fragmented personalized memory.

Conclusion

In this article we have wanted to do two things. First, we have wanted to relate the material values and the practices of writers, directors, and actors to the meaning of Chekhov in production. Secondly, we have looked at the different representations of class and history that these practices embodied in the Eyre/Griffiths and the Noble productions of *The Cherry Orchard*, despite their rhetorical similarity in the face of conventional academic readings.

We have taken a comparative 'reading formation' approach which contrasted the Griffiths/Williams formation with the Noble/ RSC conjuncture partly for reasons of space. A fuller account would be more diachronic – examining, for example, the 'performance' *disagreements* between writer, set designer, and director in Act II of the Eyre/Griffiths production; or the attempts by actors David Troughton and Sean Murray to re-establish that sense of 'change agent' intimacy between Lopakhin and Trofimov which Noble as their director was effacing. Any fuller account would thus examine the *process* of the construction of class and history sequentially (but not necessarily coherently) from pre-performance publicity for Noble's *The Cherry Orchard*, through rehearsal and performance, to the subsequent reviews and audience readings.

Notes and References

1. 'Adrian Noble talks with Peter Holland', *In Conversation: Explorations on the Stratford Season, 1995-96*, RSC, 24 January 1996. All other quotations from Noble are from this interview, except where referenced.

2. Trevor Griffiths, trans., *The Cherry Orchard, in a New English Version* (London: Pluto, 1981), p. v.

3. Interview with John Tulloch, July 1993.

4. J. Tulloch and T. Burvill, 'Chekhov: in Criticism, Performance, and Reading', Australian Research Council Large Grant, 1993-96. Currently this is being written up for a book.

5. David Mamet, quoted in *The Cherry Orchard* programme, New Theatre, 9 November–21 December 1996.

6. Mary-Anne Gifford, 'Director's Note', New Theatre programme.

7. See Anna Seymour, 'Culture and Political Change: British Radical Theatre in Recent History', *Theatre International Research*, V, No. 21 (1996), p. 11.

8. Trevor Griffiths, interviewed by John Tulloch, July 1993.

9. All interviews with actors and personnel involved with the Richard Eyre/Trevor Griffiths productions of *The Cherry Orchard* in 1977 (Nottingham Playhouse) and 1981 (BBC Television) were conducted by John Tulloch and/or Tom Burvill in 1993-94.

10. Stanton B. Garner, Jr., 'History in the Year Two: Trevor Griffiths's Danton', *New Theatre Quarterly*, XI, No. 44 (1995), p. 335.

11. Richard Eyre, interviewed by John Tulloch, July 1993.

12. It is important to emphasize that, in other respects, Trevor Griffiths was very happy with Bill Patterson's performance.

13. Trevor Griffiths, quoted in Desmond Christy, 'Back to the Barricades', *The Guardian*, 28 April 1986.

14. See Mike Poole and John Wyver, *Powerplays: Trevor Griffiths in Television* (London: BFI, 1984), p. 13-15.

15. J. Tulloch, T. Burvill, and A. Hood, 'Receptions and Appropriations: *The Cherry Orchard* in Production and Criticism', in D. Clayton, ed., *Chekhov Then and Now: the Reception of Chekhov in World Culture* (Ottawa: Peter Lang, forthcoming), p. 63-75.

16. Trevor Griffiths, lecturing at David Edgar's MA course in playwriting, University of Birmingham, 1990.

17. Trevor Griffiths, interviewed by John Tulloch, July 1993.

18. Ibid.

19. Ibid.

20. Interview with Peter Holland, January 1996.

21. Ibid.

22. Ronnie Mulryne and Margaret Shewring, *Making Space for Theatre: British Architecture and Theatre since 1958* (Stratford: Mulryne and Shewring, 1995), p. 168.

23. Interview with John Tulloch, January 1996.

24. Rod Dungate at the Swan, RSC, July 1995.

JoAnne Akalaitis
interviewed by Deborah Saivetz

Releasing the 'Profound Physicality of Performance'

In the following interview, JoAnne Akalaitis discusses her experiences as an actress and director with the Mabou Mines company; her artistic encounters with Beckett, Brecht, and Genet; her thoughts about the relationship between art and politics; and her belief in the connection between the physical and the emotional in performance. Deborah Saivetz is a director and performer who teaches in the Department of Visual and Performing Arts at the Newark Campus of Rutgers University, New Jersey. She assisted JoAnne Akalaitis on her production of John Ford's Jacobean tragedy *'Tis Pity She's a Whore* at the Goodman Theatre in Chicago, and performed in Akalaitis's workshop production of *The Mormon Project* at the Atlantic Center for the Arts in New Smyrna Beach, Florida. She had several opportunities to talk at length with Akalaitis during the months that they worked together.

JoANNE AKALAITIS is one of America's leading theatre directors. She is noted for her imagistic and sculptural approach to staging, and for a body of work ranging from original theatre pieces to adaptations of literary works to unconventional interpretations of classics. Her multi-layered and collage-like works combine text, acting, and design to create highly evocative theatrical environments.

In Akalaitis's stagings, the dramatic event is especially present in the bodies of the actors and in the scenic architecture of space, image, light, sound, and music. These compositional elements not only contribute structure and form to the work, but also convey emotion. For Akalaitis, theatrical space is psychological space and physical geography is emotional geography.

From 1970 to 1990, JoAnne Akalaitis was a member of Mabou Mines, the experimental theatre group she co-founded in New York with Lee Breuer, Ruth Maleczeh, David Warrilow, and Philip Glass. She made her directorial debut in 1975 with a fully-staged version of Samuel Beckett's radio play *Cascando*. During the early 1980s, Akalaitis branched out from her work with Mabou Mines and began directing large-scale

works at major regional theatres throughout the United States.

In May 1991, Joseph Papp, the legendary founder and producer of the New York Shakespeare Festival, named Akalaitis as his artistic associate. Three months later she was appointed Papp's successor, and upon Papp's death in the autumn of 1991 took over as artistic director of the Festival. In March 1993, after a stormy twenty-month tenure, she was dismissed by the theatre's board of directors.

JoAnne Akalaitis's directing credits include August Strindberg's *The Dance of Death* at the Arena Stage in Washington, DC; *Suddenly Last Summer* by Tennessee Williams at Connecticut's Hartford Stage; *The Rover, Leon and Lena (and Lenz)* and *The Screens* at the Guthrie Theatre in Minneapolis, Minnesota; *In the Summer House* at Lincoln Center in New York; *'Tis Pity She's a Whore* at the Goodman Theatre in Chicago; *Cymbeline, Henry IV Parts One and Two*, and *Woyzeck* at the New York Shakespeare Festival; *Dead End Kids*, Franz Xaver Kroetz's *Request Concert* (Drama Desk Award), and *Through the Leaves* with Mabou Mines; Philip Glass's *The Photographer* at the Brooklyn Academy of Music Next Wave Festival; *Endgame* and

The Balcony at American Repertory Theatre in Cambridge, Massachusetts; and *Green Card* at the Mark Taper Forum, Los Angeles.

She has been the recipient of a 1993 Obie Award for Sustained Achievement, the 1993 Edwin Booth Award, four Obie Awards for Distinguished Direction and Production, a Guggenheim Fellowship for experimental theatre, and also of Rockefeller and National Endowment for the Arts grants for playwriting. Akalaitis currently serves as co-chair of the MFA Directing Program at the Juilliard School in New York. She recently directed *The Visit* at City Opera in New York, and is currently at work on several projects, among them a theatre piece based on the life and work of Jack Kerouac, a musical about Louis Armstrong's wife, and a production of Strindberg's *A Dream Play* with advanced students from the Juilliard acting company.

Stopping, Starting, Moving

On the day that Ryszard Cieslak's obituary appeared in the New York Times[1] *you recalled that he taught you something very important about acting – that it happens in the body. You've also spoken about your belief that the essence of theatre is bodies moving in space. Would you talk a bit about the physical exercises that you do in rehearsal? Where did they come from? Did you develop them gradually, over time?*

Oh, I don't know. I just get ideas from. . . . I think they came from me.

And do they change when you work on each project?

They do.

During rehearsals for both 'Tis Pity She's a Whore and The Mormon Project workshop, you gave the actors similar tasks to explore during the exercises. The idea of 'stopping and starting', for instance.

That actually came up a couple of years ago and it became very important to me. I think at the time I was working on *Green Card* at the Taper. I invented it. Or, I didn't invent it, I *saw* it. There are certain things that are indigenous to a production or to a company, and I discover them while working.

Stopping and starting is something that actors seem to have a hard time doing. Perhaps their training somehow doesn't prepare them to work that way. There's a sense in which you ask the actor to travel from 'A' to 'C', both physically and emotionally. And that can be difficult, and even frustrating, because the actors must supply the transition, the 'B', themselves.

It *is* hard to do.

You've also referred to Genet's idea that each scene should be performed as if it were a play, in and of itself.

Yes. That was a very big influence on me. It's not that you deny transitions. Actors figure it out, they negotiate a way from one thing to the other. And they *have* to do that.

That's a very foreign thing for some actors to do.

Yes, but I think a lot of things are foreign for actors, and it's because actors have not been trained in a physical way. They've not dealt with certain physical realities or body work. Or they think they have, and it's off-putting to them. They don't understand, and I think directors often don't understand either, that performance is profoundly physical.

Do you think directors themselves should know how to move onstage? Or at least understand it?

Maybe they shouldn't have to. Maybe they shouldn't have to know how to move, or even understand how to put actors in some kind of movement ambience. But what they need to understand is that they *don't* understand it. Do you know what I mean?

That reminds me of something you've often said as you lead the slow-motion 'painting exercise': 'If you don't know what painting you're in, just make sure that you know that. That you know that you don't know.'

Scene from JoAnne Akalaitis's production of *'Tis Pity She's a Whore*, for the Goodman Theatre, Chicago (1990), with Lauren Tom as Annabella, Don Cheadle as Soranzo, and Erick Avari as Vasques. Photo: Liz Lauren.

Yes. Robert Wilson brings in this Japanese woman, this choreographer who's very in touch with all the aspects of the production, very in touch with the performers. And actually I think Bob knows a lot about movement, but he also knows how to get an expert in there to help him. I think that there are many denials among American directors. One is the denial of design. Another is the denial of the actor as an empowered, collaborative partner in the production. And the third is the denial of movement – space – the body in space.

Possessing the Space

What do you mean by 'the denial of design'? Many directors speak a great deal about design and its importance in their work.

Well, I think it's not just directors. There's an anti-visual bias in the American theatre that's been going on for a long time. And journalists try to put together this idea of the *auteur* director as a visually-oriented director because *they*, the journalists, don't understand the visual. *They're* uneducated.

They're not dealing with the amazing power of the development of design in American theatre. They think that if there's some kind of 'look' onstage it denies the playwright.

It's a very simplistic way of looking at theatre. And I think a lot of directors come at it – not because of any criticism or scholarship, but because it's basically been the way of thinking about theatre – from the point of view that the set is the background for the unfolding of events that the playwright has written. And it's so screwed-up.

It was very exciting to be around John Conklin and Pat Collins during rehearsals for 'Tis Pity She's a Whore.[2] They knew so much about the play, not simply in terms of design but dramaturgically. It seemed, though, that the actors had a lot of trouble making the transition from the rehearsal room to that huge space which is the Goodman stage.

Yes, but that's fine for the actors. Actors *should* have trouble. Actors basically are working in a very private, hermetic, deeply subjective way – which they *should* be doing. This hopefully will translate into a public, objective, physicalized way of working. The actor then has to put herself or himself into space, and that's a really hard thing to do. Actors say, 'Oh, the set, it's so hard to work on.' They all say that. They *should* say that. They *need* to say that. And then they need to get on to the next step, which is to understand that the set supports them and embraces them. And they have to figure out how to dominate. I often say that the actors have to possess the space. And they usually do.

Throughout the rehearsal process for 'Tis Pity you spoke about the feel, the sensibility, of Futurism. And you continually reminded the actors that they needed to internalize that – its rhythm, its form, its speed. This also is something that actors trained in more conventional ways rarely think about. They are used to thinking about their characters, their emotions and their private feelings.

Yes, except when you offer actors any kind of information – it could be dramaturgical information about character or some kind of historical exegesis – they love it. They really love it. I've noticed that. Some don't – some just want to work on their character. But, for the most part, they're not overwhelmed. They're grateful for information.

Why, when actors do a speed-through rehearsal, is it usually so good?[3]

I think all directors say that. It's always true. I don't know, there's something. . . . You can't *do* the play, you can't *perform* it, as a speed-through, but during a speed-through you see everything. Everything is crystallized and condensed. And it can be a joyous, exciting, competitive, collaborative experience. And actors do learn from doing speed-throughs. Because you say to them, 'Okay, well, now do it that way.' And they won't do it exactly that way, but they'll do it more that way. Whatever the beats are, you have to encounter them very quickly instead of wending your way to them. And actors like speed-throughs. Everyone likes them. You don't have to deal with the blocking, you don't have to deal with the scenery. You see the skeleton of the play but it's not just a skeleton. It's enlivened. It's filled out.

Differences: Beckett and Genet

You've mentioned that Oliver Sacks's book Awakenings *has been very important for you. Could you speak more about that?*

It's this idea of being locked into. . . . I'm trying to figure out what it really means, because there's something about it that captures my imagination and, in some way, I have to deal with it in my aesthetics of theatre. And I think part of it is that you sort of run towards something, and then you get stopped and locked and then paralyzed. And you keep trying and trying and trying to get out of it.

I started with it in *Endgame*, for which it was specifically, thematically relevant. And it made a lot of sense for certain characters, especially in Beckett. The character of Clov, for instance. And then it made a lot of sense in *Leon and Lena*. And I find it often makes a lot of sense. You're stopped, and then you're released, and then you're sort of hurtled, self-propelled, into space. And then something else stops you. And then you're released again. Or then you're transfixed.

All of these are images that are in Sacks's book. I think it has a lot to do with Beckett, but I don't think it has a lot to do with Shakespeare, thematically. But it does have a lot to do with an actor understanding something that could be very dangerous and on the edge and, movement-wise, chaotic.

How did you become interested in Genet?

Well, I think everyone's interested in Genet. I can't even remember how I discovered Genet. Genet is simply a great twentieth-century writer, and at some point around the 'sixties he was in my life. I think I saw *The Maids* at the Actors Workshop in San Francisco and I saw *The Blacks* in New York. And a lot of people I talk to, through the years, saw *The Blacks* and remember it as a very important theatre event. I saw *Endgame*, I saw Genet – and those events were really big.

You've referred to Endgame *as one of the greatest, if not the greatest, modern plays ever written. And you've been involved with a lot of Beckett's work, both independently and with Mabou Mines. Is he a writer that you're particularly attracted to, on a personal level?*

I've never been involved with Beckett except personally. And there's nobody like Beckett. The interesting thing to me is the difference between Genet and Beckett. On the one hand, Beckett is very classical and ordered and intellectual, in the best sense of all of those words. And Genet is very Greek – classical in a different way. And sort of an adolescent, like a naughty adolescent. You know, I think Genet has a lot to say to us now. He has so much to say to us. He's a great poet. And Beckett is a great poet. In some way I'm not interested in working on Beckett, but in another way I am. I would love to work on *Waiting for Godot* or *Happy Days*. With Beckett you just get back to . . . poetry.

Beckett and Genet are often anthologized together in terms of the history of the French avant-garde.

They're completely different.

Beckett is technically very difficult.

He is, yes. But Genet is technically difficult, too. And you don't really know it because there's this kind of exuberance. On one level, there's all this high poetry, this overly baroque poetry. And on the other level, there's this kind of natural, scatological, trashy talk. What the actor has to do to negotiate between those two is amazing. I think *Endgame* is *the* modern masterpiece. But I think *The Screens* is the play of the century. I'm not quite sure what I'm saying when I say that.

Dealing with Brecht

You've said that you dislike Brecht.

I shouldn't say that. I have profound reactions against Brecht. And it's complicated. What I think has not happened yet in the American theatre, and maybe also not in the English theatre, is that no one has figured out who Brecht is in our theatrical lives. Nobody knows what to do with Brecht. Certainly I think Brecht is a great theatre poet, and a great poet. I'm very attracted to the early plays like *Baal* and *In the Jungle of Cities*. Those are my favourite plays.

I went to the Berliner Ensemble, where I saw the great Brecht masterpieces – *Mother Courage, Good Soldier Schweik, The Threepenny Opera, Coriolanus*. That was really long ago and, at the time, I was willing to be wowed. And it was a time to be wowed. But, there's no way to ignore the fact that Brecht had a very clear political agenda which to many of us, at this time, is abhorrent. It's almost like a Stalinist thing. And in some plays – like *Arturo Ui* which is a delightful play – the level of the polemic is so naive I wouldn't even know how to direct those plays. And then there are other plays, like *Galileo* and *Mother Courage,* which are basically Broadway hits: they're very commercial plays written for some kind of star. And then there's his early poetry.

But I think, when you deal with the heart of Brecht, it is a mistake to ignore his politics. Because he was a political man. That's what his plays are about. And for all of us to say, well, we can do these plays without dealing with his politics, in some way seems ignorant.

It seems naive of us.

And that whole idea about Brechtian acting is not a new idea. I think that the alienation effect is basically a Greek idea. It's very, very classical. You see yourself doing something, and you sort of refine it while you're doing it, and you put it out into space and communicate something – which is another step, another level – towards the audience. For Brecht, *that* was political. And that seems to me extraordinarily naive on his part. It's a great acting idea, but to use it politically is very, very naive.

The more I talk about it, I'm sort of irritated with Brecht. And then you deal with Genet, whose politics are so perverse and so chaotic and so insane, and whose poetry is also so perverse and so chaotic and so insane. . . . In the twentieth century, the kind of poetry that we may really have to deal with is Genet's poetry. Genet's poetry deals with the Third World. And he is the only major contemporary writer I can think of who has taken a stand in the Third World.

In some ways Beckett – which is not to put him down – and Brecht both seem kind of rarefied. They're very much from the European tradition. Genet literally took the leap in that he *lived* among Palestinians in Jordan and places like that, underground, for many, many years when he was not writing plays. And there's something very interesting about him not being a part of the literary world, even though he was a great poet, but being a part of the real world in his own screwed-up, wild, and crazy way.

It's interesting to see how that informs theatre because what's happening in the world now is that there are a lot of people who are dying of AIDS. Like Ethyl Eichelberger – I don't know if you know about this, but he committed suicide.[4] And there are a lot of homeless people. And these are the people that Genet embraced in his life – in his life *style* – and managed to put into his writing. In some ways, he's so completely contemporary.

I don't know how you get these people in. And that shouldn't be anyone's mandate, it really shouldn't. But I don't know how you can do theatre now without dealing with . . . everything. With this epidemic, with all this violence, with all these people being shot on the streets of New York, with this global ecological nightmare that is descending on us minute by minute. It's not that you have to do plays about it. But it simply has to be there.

Sometimes it seems that, as actors and simply as human beings, our frame of reference is so small. It's easy to insulate oneself.

But I don't think that actors *are* insulated. I think that they're people like us. They listen to National Public Radio and they watch television. It's that they have been programmed to separate their work from that kind of consciousness. And you can't put it in every play: it doesn't belong in every play, it probably doesn't even belong in *any* play. But if you're not working with people for whom the bottom line is some kind of social reality, then you're not working. Then you're not doing it.

Questions of Suffering – and of Power

Beckett received the Nobel Prize because he wrote about human suffering. Although I suppose he didn't live it in the way that Genet lived it.

Yes, but Beckett *did*, because he was part of the Resistance. He was a very brave person, he was wounded in the Resistance. I think Beckett did live it. And he lived it in an entirely different political world, which

Scenes from two productions by JoAnne Akalaitis. Top: Lauren Tom and Jo Harvey Allen in *Leon and Lena (and Lenz)*, for the Guthrie Theatre, 1987 (photo: Joe Giannetti). Bottom: Jesse Borrego as Giovanni and Lauren Tom as Annabella in *'Tis Pity She's a Whore* for the Goodman Theatre, 1990 (photo: Liz Lauren).

existed almost a generation before the world that Genet lived in. Genet has truly lived it in the modern world. Right at this instant, we are at war in the Middle East. Genet would love that guy – the King of Iraq. There's something about Genet that would really get off on him, because he's this macho, Arab nationalist.

You know, we're living in a dream world. We don't realize that there are Arabs all over the world, including in Detroit and Chicago, who are saying, 'Right on! We don't care about Kuwait. We're Arab nationalists. Everyone has said we've been dogs for hundreds of years, and now suddenly we're on the front page of the *New York Times*, and we want that and we need it!'

The genius of Mabou Mines was that everyone was in power. And that *was* the genius of the company – that everyone had power. Some people less than others, but there is simply nothing like that. And I don't think there ever will be. This group of people came together, and certain people were very articulate and very domineering and others weren't, but I think the way it shook down is that, in some strange way, everybody got their say and everybody got to do what they needed to do.

I was talking about that at the Public Theatre. If Joe Papp likes something that I don't like, or if he hates something that I like, what do you do about it? And the thing that you do about it is that you allow it to happen. I think that's what Mabou Mines did. There were things that certain people were doing that other people thought were awful, but the unspoken contract was that you got to do whatever you wanted to do. And it's quite a good way of working.

And if somebody didn't like what you happened to be working on, they didn't have to work on it with you?

No. But that is not the way artistic organizations are run. Basically, there's an artistic vision that says, 'You're on the wrong track with this, you have to get back on track', or, 'We've got to cancel this', or, 'You can't do this.'

You mean, the person or people in power –

Yes, but it's a good kind of power, too. Because the reason people run these institutions is not because they're idiots or maniacs. It's because they have some kind of vision. It's because they believe in theatre and they want to do something.

But not even a company like the Wooster Group was as democratic as Mabou Mines.

No, Liz LeCompte is the Artistic Director of the Wooster Group, she's the head of the Wooster Group. And the Wooster Group is, from what I can tell, very collaborative in their workings, but basically, from the public's point of view and from the company's point of view, it's run by one person. That's fine. In Mabou Mines, the director has always been the director. But, really, in its internal workings Mabou Mines functioned as a consensus mechanism. And whatever the outside world saw it as, that's how it worked.

Against the Conditioned Actor

When you speak about the actors in Mabou Mines being 'empowered' – which is a word that's so bandied about today – are you referring to the fact that they were free to work on whatever they wanted to work on?

It's not just that. I think that the revolution Mabou Mines created for actors was that they were empowered to speak out about all the aspects of a production, including design. And, in one sense, that was very, very tiresome. But, on the other hand, there's nothing like it. I actually think that design-wise Mabou Mines is quite weak. I'm being sort of ruthlessly objective. I know that Mabou Mines is known for its visual sensibility and it does have that, but I think the design has been not quite as strong as the acting, as the sense of performance.

The thing is, there were no designers. There were these sort of artists, or whatever, and they didn't really know anything about theatre. All that was great, and that was its own kind of revolution. It was like a stepping-stone in history which designers now can use for their own work. But the greatest thing was not just that the actors in Mabou Mines went on to be directors and playwrights – it was how powerful actors were in a piece.

I've seen that kind of 'unempowered' behaviour on the part of actors, that kind of deferential behaviour amongst actors who are talented, intelligent, and aware. It's sad that so much of that kind of conditioning goes on.

It is. And that's the way that the system works. Actors go to Hollywood. And it's very interesting that now they all become directors. They're smart, they realize where the power is. Because the power in theatre is held by directors and producers. That's where it's at unless you're a major star. And it happens all the time that stars dictate how a play is cast and who directs it.

A lot of people object to that, but I'm not so sure whether it's objectionable. I don't know. It's objectionable to me personally because I insist on controlling the whole production. At the same time, it has to be very collaborative. But those things are not mutually exclusive. It's an exciting, amazing kind of tension. People are helping me, and collaborating together, and giving me and the piece their own individual artistic history, and yet I am putting it all together. And basically directing it, in the simplest sense of what directing is.

You referred to the physical exercises we did in rehearsal as 'actor research'. And yet you'd sometimes see an image from those exercises and actually use it in the piece. Or maybe try it out and then discard it. Is that an example of what you're talking about? Because that was our own personal exploration.

Yes. Do you think that violates the actor . . . ?

No, not at all. Because even though you asked us simultaneously to work from the inside and see ourselves from the outside, you could see us from the outside in a different way.

Well, yes. I mean what I say with most of those exercises – that it's for the actors. Sometimes I get very bored and zone out. And other times I do the exercise myself, in my imagination. And then other times I do that *and* really look. And there are always great things, it's always great. It's amazing what actors do. Nobody could do better than actors in their work, in being inventive.

We had this casting discussion about Falstaff in the *Henry* plays. It may be that a big star will play Falstaff. And I said to the casting department, 'You have to tell these people – and I'm very happy to have a big star or a minor star – that there are no exceptions. I work the way I do. Everyone has to lie down on the floor and everyone has to stand up. Everyone has to do these exercises. No matter who that person is, she or he has to do these exercises, and there *are* no exceptions, and that's the way I work.'

Physicality, Emotion – and Not Pretending

When we were doing the 'attraction and repulsion' exercise, you'd often say, 'Now, remember, this is purely physical. This is not psychological.' And I would hear that and think to myself, 'Okay, I'll just keep it physical', but something inside of me couldn't help being activated simply by performing that physical action of going toward or away from someone.

Yes, I think the physical *is* the psychological. That's what Bob Wilson said many years ago – that the mechanical is the emotional, or something like that. And, for me, the exercises are not about creating plays, or improvisational situations or scenes. Certainly, doing the exercise *is* psychological, it's absolutely psychological, but to deal with the physical is such a primary, basic, and, for many actors, novel experience that it's important to stay glommed on to it.

Otherwise, the exercise becomes narrative, and I think that it's very important in acting to be pre-narrative – in all these plays, the Shakespeare plays, the Chekhov plays, to be open to some kind of physicalized state that does not define what the actual physicality of the character is too early in the rehearsal process, but to be in a kind of primeval, subconscious, unconscious state that is open to the whole world, or *worlds*, of the play.

So that's the background, sort of the base of it. And then when you go on to do the really articulated work, you always have that to fall back on. And it's very secure because it's a completely primitive physicality. And out of that you make it really detailed for the performance. And you *have* to make it detailed for the performance.

Something that has been meaningful to me, as a performer, and that has been reinforced by working with you, is the importance of not pretending. It's a double-edged thing because, in a sense, you are always pretending in the theatre. Many theatre artists and scholars have spoken about this paradox, but, personally, it's very difficult for me to perform when I feel obligated to pretend onstage. I really enjoy working on Beckett, for instance, because I don't feel that I have to do any pretending. Likewise, I found it very easy not to have to pretend while doing the physical exercises. When you are required during the exercises to concentrate on the actual physical surroundings of the rehearsal room, to be aware of your own body and the other bodies around you, you are in fact operating in that pre-narrative realm because you're dealing with your knee and this other person's body and this wall. And even when you begin to allow your character to seep in, you're still responding to this floor and this arm. And that's another thing that's not often focused upon, both in the training of actors and in the theatre itself – dealing with what's really happening in front of you at each moment.

Oh, I know exactly what you're talking about. I am stunned by what theatres are doing. I don't understand what directors are doing. I don't understand how directors are talking to actors. I don't know what's going on. There are simply no ideas about how to put it together. Basically people are either doing plays or making these grand career moves like, 'I'm doing this piece and I need to have this actress be in it.'

It seems that putting one's attention on the physical often allows what's inside to free up and express itself.

It's a very simple thing. It's the inside and outside coming together. There really is nothing like it. And, oddly enough, very few actors can do it. I never thought of that – it's weird, isn't it – that very few actors actually do it, put the two together. I thought that Denzel Washington was doing it. I went to the opening of *Richard III* the other night, and the critics were so mean to him, and I thought, 'Why should this really, really talented guy ever want to do a play again?' He was actually doing something onstage, he was actually working. And his physical work was so interesting.

Did you read the *New York Times* review? Mel Gussow said, 'He contorted his body so much that he kept talking over his shoulder.' Which he did. It was so great. I was really impressed by the way he used his body. He's an important American actor, and there he was trying to do something very important. He's going to get better and better. He was doing something onstage. He was talking and he was making sense. He walked onstage and I thought, 'Hey, here's a guy who's working.' And they just shot him down.

Notes and References

1. Ryszard Cieslak was a member of Grotowski's Polish Laboratory Theatre until it ceased touring in 1980, and is best remembered for his performance in *The Constant Prince* and *Apocalypsis cum Figuris*. His obituary appeared in the *New York Times* on 16 June 1990.

2. Conklin designed the sets and Collins designed the lights for the Goodman Theatre production of *'Tis Pity She's a Whore*.

3. Toward the end of the rehearsal period, Akalaitis scheduled a number of 'speed-throughs' during which the entire company of actors would sit on the floor in a circle and rapidly, with a tremendous amount of energy and concentration, speak the text of the play.

4. Ethyl Eichelberger, a leading actor with Charles Ludlam's Ridiculous Theatre Company, had been diagnosed with, and was suffering the effects of, the AIDS virus when he committed suicide during the summer of 1990.

Susan F. Clark

Solo Black Performance before the Civil War: Mrs. Stowe, Mrs. Webb, and 'The Christian Slave'

In contemporary culture, an 'Uncle Tom' has become so derided a figure of complicity in racism that it is perhaps only with difficulty, and a corrective historicist awareness, that we can come to acknowledge both the good intentions and the undeniable effectiveness of Harriet Beecher Stowe's original – a novel in which, interestingly, women play no less prominent a part than black characters. Indeed, it is likely that the proliferating stage adaptations of Mrs. Stowe's novel were largely responsible for creating the stereotype Uncle Tom in a popular imagination on which such melodramatized accounts had a lasting impact: and it was partly in response to such perversions that Mrs. Stowe herself set out to dramatize her novel. The result, *The Christian Slave*, has remained relatively unknown not least because of the premature death of its solo performer, Mary Webb – herself a pioneer among black performers who achieved recognition from white audiences. In the following article, Susan F. Clark examines the play in its contemporary context, contrasts it both with other stage versions and with the seminal novel, and examines the relationship between its black performer and her audiences. Susan F. Clark is Assistant Professor of Theatre History at Smith College, Massachusetts, and is currently working on a full-length study of interpretations of *Uncle Tom's Cabin* on the American stage.

BY 1855, the battle lines that would stake out the American Civil War were being drawn. Each political compromise aimed at avoiding confrontation, such as the Kansas-Nebraska Act, spurred further discussion and heightened emotional response to the issue of slavery. In the midst of these controversies and debates, *Uncle Tom's Cabin*, Harriet Beecher Stowe's popular novel, was frequently used to argue both the pro- and anti-slavery viewpoints.

The proliferation of Uncle Tom characters on the stages of dozens of cities accelerated the public's familiarity with the story, although the plays were often riddled with inaccuracies and distortions. In 1855, Harriet Beecher Stowe wrote a pointedly revised version of *Uncle Tom's Cabin*, a dramatization entitled *The Christian Slave*. It was the only play her Calvinist objections to the theatre would ever allow her to pen, and she designated it 'expressly for . . . Mrs. Mary E. Webb', a mulatto dramatic reader

who had just begun her professional career. Some scholars, dismissing this play as merely another example of Mrs. Stowe's well-documented philanthropy, attribute its creation to the authoress's desire to assist Mary Webb with her career.[1] However, both the emphatic revisions of the text and the unusual act of designating a single person as the specific reader for the piece suggests that there was more to the writing of *The Christian Slave* than a gesture of generosity.

The change in title is the first indication that Mrs. Stowe fully intended to write a play that was *not* associated with those currently playing the boards. Nor was *The Christian Slave* the first of Mrs. Stowe's retaliations to 'the popular impressions . . . produced by the reading and acting of *Uncle Tom's Cabin*'.[2] In 1853, she had joined forces with leading anti-slavery figures to help organize a series of lectures that would help to clarify the message of the book. In 1855, using this same anti-slavery lecture series as a forum, Mrs. Stowe and Mrs. Webb capitalized on the resonance created by a dignified, intelligent black woman reader portraying the reconfigured characters of the novel.

Streamlining the action of *Uncle Tom's Cabin* to a single, unified plot, *The Christian Slave* gives prominence to the slave and women characters who are all but forgotten, except as comic or minor figures, in the unauthorized play versions. This shift in gender and racial dynamics resonates in both the text and in the selection of the reader. In this way, *The Christian Slave* represents an astute awareness of its own performative qualities, and of the collaboration of author and performer to create a work that combines art and politics in equal measures.

In pre-Civil War America, power and privilege rested almost exclusively in the hands of white men. In the male-dominated commercial theatre world, this patriarchal ideology was commonly reflected and reinforced on the stage. In adapting *Uncle Tom's Cabin* to the stage, the message and intent of Mrs. Stowe's novel was frequently altered. By joining forces, Mrs. Stowe and Mrs. Webb created a powerful one-woman show that undoubtedly 'caused considerable astonishment to any gentleman of the Southern States' – or any other state – who happened to see it.[3]

Mrs. Stowe's Motivations

To date, there is no precise documentation to suggest what motivated Harriet Beecher Stowe in writing *The Christian Slave*. Her biographers say little about the publication of the play, and provide no indication of Mrs. Stowe's reasons for so substantially revising *Uncle Tom's Cabin*. It has been suggested that, as with Mrs. Stowe's assistance to Elizabeth Greenfield, a vocalist who became known as 'The Black Swan', *The Christian Slave* was the product of Mrs. Stowe's benevolence.[4] The writing of a full-length play, however, hugely surpasses the gifts of clothing, money, and letters of introduction that Mrs. Stowe provided to the many others who sought her assistance. It seems likely that Mrs. Stowe saw an opportunity to help both Mrs. Webb and herself when she set about the task of revising *Uncle Tom's Cabin*. The book had aroused intense feelings around the already hotly debated issue of slavery. Criticisms of the book and its authoress had come from both Northern and Southern quarters, from abolitionists as well as from pro-slavery advocates.

Critics from the South accused Harriet Beecher Stowe of dishonesty and misrepresentation in writing a novel depicting scenes of Southern plantation life. *The Picayune* dated 2 April 1853 succinctly made the point of many Southerners when it riddled: 'Why is Mrs. Stowe an admirer of the poet Akenside? Because she shows by *Uncle Tom's Cabin* that she delights to indulge in the Pleasures of Imagination.'[5]

Mrs. Stowe's first attempt to defend the beleaguered *Uncle Tom's Cabin* was the publication of the *Key to Uncle Tom's Cabin* (1853), a collection of articles, advertisements, and testimonials 'proving' the truth behind the incidents in her novel. The hardship and suffering of slaves, the practice of separating children from their parents, the importance of the market value of slaves, and other aspects of Southern life were described in vivid, if belated, documentation. However, in addition to arousing still further criticism, the publication of the *Key* thrust Mrs. Stowe prominently into the limelight as a newly acclaimed authority on the subject of slavery.

The reluctant spokeswoman was also criticized by abolitionists. The well-known William Lloyd Garrison used the pages of his anti-slavery paper, *The Liberator*, to point out the racist message of the novel:

That all the slaves of the South ought, 'if smitten on the cheek, to turn the other also' – to repudiate all carnal weapons, shed no blood, 'be obedient to their masters', wait for a peaceful deliverance, and abstain from all insurrectionary movements – is everywhere taken for granted, because the VICTIMS ARE BLACK. . . . Nothing can be plainer than that such conduct is obligatory upon them; and when, through the operation of divine grace, they are enabled to manifest a spirit like this, it is acknowledged to be worthy of great commendation, as in the case of 'Uncle Tom'.[6]

This early premonition of the use that the twentieth century would make of the epithet 'Uncle Tom' caused Harriet Beecher Stowe perhaps more distress than any other critical comment. A published letter from Henry C. Wright, alluding to the novel's depiction of George Harris's flight to Liberia, compares Harriet Beecher Stowe's fiction to the premises of the American Colonization Society:

The author's arguments . . . are but the echoes of the arguments, by which the negro-haters of this republic have for thirty years been seeking to drive the free coloured people from this land; and the author, in repeating them . . . will stand first on the list of the unscrupulous tyrants, of despisers of humanity, and blasphemers against God.[7]

The Novel Melodramatized

In addition to the thousands of people who had read *Uncle Tom's Cabin*, thousands more were enjoying the melodramatic spectacles of Uncle Tom on the popular stage. Taking advantage of the absence of copyright laws, dozens of playwrights appropriated the characters, events, and title of the novel in their various plays, all claiming to express the true meaning of the authoress. As one newspaper writer commented:

The penalty of a good novel is a poor play. Every person who achieves a success in the literature of romance must expect to endure martyrdom upon the stage, and the extent of a novelist's popularity may be safely found upon the degree of zeal which the playwrights manifest in torturing his conceptions upon the dramatic rack.[8]

By the time she wrote *The Christian Slave*, Harriet Beecher Stowe's theatrical martyrdom was well under way. Baltimore, Richmond, Chicago, Albany, Boston, Providence, Philadelphia, Hartford, and New York all hosted adaptations of the famous novel. Part minstrel show, part melodrama, the *Uncle Tom's Cabin* shows aroused strong emotions in audiences who wept, booed, laughed, and cheered at the stereotyped characters, sensationalized events, musical interludes, and scenic splendours before them. *Uncle Tom's Cabin* had become a theatrical hitching post to which any dramatist, manager, or actor might tie his fortunes.

Though citing Mrs. Stowe's novel as the source of their dramatizations, the plays frequently interpolated characters, exaggerated actions, and manipulated the message of the novel to placate the political and moral views of their audiences. *The New York Herald*, eager to keep all anti-slavery sentiments away from the public eye, pointed to the ludicrous embellishments and lack of political message of the Aiken version in an attempt to deter audiences:

If we were to attempt to describe succinctly the materials of which the drama is composed, we should say that stale jokes and vulgar balderdash comprised about one half, and a very sad mimicry of religion the other half, of the six acts in which it is represented. Slavery is only incidentally alluded to. The strong points made by Mrs. Stowe in the argumentative portion of her work are judiciously avoided.[9]

At the age of seventy-five, Mrs. Stowe would still recall one of the few performances she attended, where, 'after remaining a short time and seeing the many inaccuracies, I did not care to remain through the evening'.[10]

Mrs. Stowe's true intention in writing *Uncle Tom's Cabin* may be perceived in her claim that God had written the novel, not she. *The Christian Slave* is Mrs. Stowe's clarification of *Uncle Tom's Cabin* and her rebuttal to her critics and to the stage. Research has yet to discover whether it was the happy coincidence of her introduction to Mrs. Webb and her dramatic abilities that inspired Mrs. Stowe to retaliate in a similarly dramatic format. Nevertheless, there is an ironic justice in Mrs. Stowe's act of fighting fire with fire, and of defending the integrity of *Uncle Tom's Cabin* by using the very same medium that had made a minstrelized mockery of him.

There is little background information on Mary Webb, the single fullest source being the 'Biographical Sketch' written by her own husband, Frank, and first published in the London edition of *The Christian Slave* (1856). The progeny of an escaped slave and a wealthy Spanish gentleman named Espartero, Mary Webb was born in New Bedford, Massachusetts, in 1828. Having 'enjoyed comfortable circumstances and a good education', her marriage at the age of seventeen to Frank J. Webb, a free-born Philadelphian, provided her with an introduction to the famous Forten family and to Philadelphia society.[11]

The Debut of Mary Webb

After the collapse of Frank Webb's business, Mary, determining to turn 'her marked elocutionary powers to some practical account', studied with A. A. Apthorp, a professor of elocution in Philadelphia.[12] Cognizant of the difficulties 'which beset the path of every aspirant for public distinction', Mary Webb was also acutely aware that she 'must storm the ramparts of prejudice' if she was to 'wring from the unwilling lips of the despisers of her race a confession of merit'.[13]

Mary Webb debuted as a dramatic reader on 19 April 1855 in Philadelphia, with a programme that included poetry as well as dramatic verses. Although the biographical sketch of Mary Webb insists that, following this performance, 'the audience lost the mulatto in the artiste' and 'genius had become the conqueror of prejudice,' Charlotte Forten Grimke's diary entry for 19 November 1855 reflects the level of prejudice to be found even amongst well-wishers and abolitionists:

This evening attended Mrs. Webb's readings; they were principally from Shakespeare. I was not very much pleased. I wish coloured persons would not attempt to do anything of the kind unless they can compare favourably with others. But I know I should not presume to criticize, and most sincerely hope if she has talent, it may be cultivated, and that she may succeed in her vocation, reflecting credit upon herself and her race.[14]

Despite this criticism, by the fall of 1855 Mrs. Webb had earned the sobriquet of the 'Black Siddons', after the famous British actress, Sarah Siddons. Exactly when or how Mary Webb came to Mrs. Stowe's attention is unclear, but the 'Biographical Sketch' does indicate that it was early in her career:

A few months subsequent to her debut, she had the good fortune to procure an introduction to Mrs. H. Beecher Stowe, a woman admired for her genius and loved for her philanthropy on both sides of the Atlantic. Aided by her assistance, and influenced and encouraged by her regard, she pursued her dramatic studies during the summer succeeding her great debut with great ardour; and at the opening of the winter season she reappeared in Boston at the Fremont Temple and read, for the first time, *The Christian Slave*, a dramatization of *Uncle Tom's Cabin*, which was prepared by Mrs. Stowe expressly for Mrs. Webb's readings. It was produced to an audience of 3,500 people, one of the largest ever assembled in the Temple, and met with unbounded applause. She subsequently read it to large audiences in different parts of the Northern States, and always with success.[15]

That Mrs. Stowe and Mrs. Webb shared similar political sympathies is clear from the letter of introduction written by the author to Mr. and Mrs. Edward Baines:

[Mrs. Webb's] success . . . is attested by hundreds of notices, written by the most competent critics in this country. Indeed it has been so great as to cause even Pro-Slavery Lyceums to solicit her services in their course which have been closed to persons of her complexion – by the prejudices to colour so strongly prevalent in this country. . . . Her success in England will benefit the Anti-Slavery Cause in this country by showing of what the race is capable and how much talent had conceded among those with whom she is identified.[16]

Frank Webb, writing in the introduction to *The Christian Slave*, echoes Mrs. Stowe's sentiments regarding the potential positive effect of Mrs. Webb's success as a reader:

Mrs. Webb's success . . . will serve a nobler end. . . . It will prove that the right which has been claimed for us, by the friends of our race, to stand side by side with our fair-skinned oppressors . . . is not made without strong foundation for its support. When that time shall come . . . then will my oppressed fellow countrymen prove . . . that the tinge on their brow is not the badge of inferiority . . . . then genius will no longer be

Mary Webb giving her performance of *The Christian Slave* in the hall of Stafford House. An engraving from *The Illustrated London News* of 2 August 1856.

considered as the exclusive attribute of one race or another, but a gift distributed with an impartial hand by our beneficent common Father.[17]

In addition to advancing the anti-slavery cause, both women personally had much to gain from the successful readings of *The Christian Slave*. Mary Webb's readings gave Frank Webb the time and financial resources to complete his novel, *The Garies and Their Friends*, the first book to be published by an African American in the United States. And while there is no indication that Mrs. Stowe benefited financially from *The Christian Slave*, her dramatization reasserted the integrity of her novel in a powerful and public way. Together, the two women took a small step towards breaking down the barriers of prejudice.

Despite its title, *Uncle Tom's Cabin* is concerned primarily with the dilemmas of white men acting in a society created and

343

maintained by them. Preoccupied with debates about the 'negro problem,' the novel presents Uncle Tom as little more than a passive chattel that white men may sell, exchange, abandon, or abuse, depending on the needs or whims of their fluctuating circumstances.

Restoring Black and Female Viewpoints

The stage versions reflect this same preoccupation with the problems of the white society in dealing with 'the peculiar institution' of the South, and focus the attention on the sensational events that occur because of 'the problem'. Slave escapes, dehumanizing auctions, and inter-racial sexual intimidation, floggings, and even death serve as emotional highlights to sadden, horrify, and titillate white audiences.

George Aiken's script, *Uncle Tom's Cabin; or, Life Among the Lowly* is perhaps the most faithful in reproducing the interwoven plots of the novel and is today considered to be the 'standard' playscript. Relegating the action and debates of white males to the background, *The Christian Slave* inverts the racial and gender dynamics of the stage versions, and restores the black and female points of view that are distinctly minoritized in the plays. A simple chart comparing the allocation of speaking roles in the two plays will illustrate the distinction between the Aiken and Stowe dramatizations:[18]

	Aiken	*Stowe*
White male characters	13	5
Black male characters	4	8
White female characters	3	4
Black female characters	5	10
Total characters	25	27

The Aiken version has a total of 17 male roles, over 75 per cent of which represent white characters. Stowe's play reduces the total number of male speaking roles to 13, with the majority, 61 per cent, delineating black male characters. *The Christian Slave* lists parts for 14 female characters, almost twice the number of Aiken's script. Stowe's black women characters outnumber Aiken's by an exact ratio of two to one. In total, *The Christian Slave* nearly doubles the representation of *both* women and black characters (male and female) by contrast with the standard Aiken script. In performance, the persona of Mary Webb visually and vocally reinforced the gender and/or racial characteristics of 22 out of *The Christian Slave's* 27 characters.

A similar shift in emphasis can be seen by comparing the selection of incidents and locations in the two scripts. *The Christian Slave* is written in three acts, compared to the more broadly sweeping six acts of the Aiken drama. Each act represents a separate segment of Uncle Tom's life. Act I takes place in or near Uncle Tom's cabin, on the Shelby property; Act II is set at St. Clare's plantation; and Act III is located entirely at Legree's slave-farm.

Tom is the only character (with the exception of the young George Shelby, who reappears at the end of the play as a grown man) who is present in all three acts, and each act closes with the unspoken but implied question, 'What will happen to Uncle Tom?' Tom is distinctly the central figure of this drama, his changing circumstances and his response to them providing the structural unity and thematic thesis of the play.

By contrast, the title of Aiken's *Uncle Tom's Cabin* might almost appear as a misnomer as its six acts career from location to location, with only one brief scene taking place in the famous cabin. In attempting to give equal weight to the stories of Uncle Tom, Eliza and George, little Eva, and Ophelia and Topsy, the play has all the attractions of a thrilling amusement park ride through the chamber of horrors: ice-blocked rivers, seedy taverns, gothic chambers, auction blocks, and whipping posts are among the scenic images that reinforce the overall melodrama of the action.

The Christian Slave deliberately downplays or eliminates the sensational events of the novel. As in the book, the emphasis is firmly on the issues rather than the actions. Most of the scenes take place in comfortably domestic environments: kitchens, living rooms, boudoirs, and dining rooms. Consistent with the 'cult of true womanhood' prevalent in the mid-nineteenth century, women and their domains provide the moral centre from which the action radiates.

Appropriately, the women's actions and thoughts are emphasized in all three acts. In Act I, the focus is placed on Mrs. Shelby's cunning resistance to the tyrant Haley; in Act II, Ophelia and little Eva's pricking of St. Clare's conscience echoes Tom's attempts at converting his owner; and in Act III Cassy's nurturing of both Tom and Emmeline, and her aggressive anger and action in response to Legree's villainy, make her a mother-hero. In virtually all of the scenes, women are the major characters who fulfil roles as moral guideposts, comforters, domestic engineers, and when necessary militant resistors.

The Christian Slave provides two contrasting examples of black survival in the characters of Tom and Cassy. Both characters, more sinned against than sinning, react according to the strength of their Christian belief. Tom, the Christian slave of the title, focuses his attention on the rewards of the next world, and his actions are motivated by his wish to fulfil the wishes of his heavenly Father.

He is first seen in his role as a devoted father and husband, in the domestic setting of his own home on the Shelby's farm. In St. Clare's household, he serves as a spiritual comrade to little Eva and a moral touchstone for the doubts of his master. Finally, in the last act, he is 'Father Tom', hearing Cassy's confession of guilt and offering her paternalistic guidance when her human endurance is at an end. His dying words, 'Who – who – who – shall separate – us from – the – the – love of Christ? LOVE! LOVE! LOVE OF CHRIST!' attest to the inability of his earthly trials to part him from his heavenly Creator and provide the key to his ability to survive.[19]

Cassy, by contrast, is uncertain of God's love for her as she is pushed to the end of her maternal and womanly limits. She is an angry young woman, outraged that her dreams of domestic bliss and motherhood have been snatched from her. The antithesis of the passive 'black victim' that William Lloyd Garrison was so critical of, Cassy illustrates the drastic result of facing desperation and despair without the redeeming power of faith.

Though Cassy appears only in the final act of the play, seven of the last eight scenes are devoted to her narrative, climaxing in a four-page monologue. In this confessional speech, Cassy relates the tale of her love for her white master, the children she bore him, and the family's separation into slavery. Recounting the pain of seeing her children in the hands of cruel masters, she determines never to allow that pain to be inflicted again. The emotional climax of her speech must have wrung the heart of every mother in the audience:

Captain Stuart was very kind to me. . . . In the course of a year I had a son born. O, that child! how I loved it! . . . But I had made up my mind – yes, I had – I would never again let a child live to grow up! So, when he was two weeks old, I took the little fellow in my arms, and I gave him laudanum. It didn't hurt him; it made him so quiet, and I held him close – close to my bosom and he slept to death![20]

The desperation that causes Cassy to kill her child erupts into additional violence at the end of the play. Cassy is kept from killing Legree only by the hand of Uncle Tom, who is bound by the laws of another world. Through Tom and Cassy, Mrs. Stowe restricts her portrayal of the effects of slavery to binary opposites, one leading to Christian acceptance unto death and the other to rebellion and resistance. Conspicuously missing is the story of George Harris and his family, and any mention of a conciliatory colonization plan.

Mary Webb and 'The Christian Slave'

Though some assume that *The Christian Slave* was writen only as a closet drama, Harriet Beecher Stowe's intention that the piece be performed is without question. Though the play lacks the dramatic action and spectacle of the more highly popularized versions, songs, stage directions, and details of stage business are included in the script, indicating at least a nod towards theatrical convention. The title page declares the work to be a dramatization, specifying it 'for . . . readings'. The restriction of the readings to a single individual may have been Mrs. Stowe's attempt to retain a measure of control over the piece (something for which her experience at the hands of the theatre managers in particular had taught her the desperate need).

Anticipating the limited attention span of an audience for an unstaged reading, the edition inscribed by Mrs. Stowe to Mary Webb indicates cuts to be made in the script for the readings.[21] A total of nine scenes are thus indicated for deletion in performance. Posters and advertisements announce the running time of *The Christian Slave* to be ninety minutes; the reading of the script in its entirety would have extended this to well over two hours.

Mary Webb's great success in reading *The Christian Slave* is evidenced by newspaper accounts, advertisements, and reviews from 1855 and 1856. *The Christian Slave*'s debut in Boston was given on the same day that the first published edition was advertised for sale, and newspaper announcements for the event advised audiences that it would be 'especially desirable' for audience members to purchase a printed copy of *The Christian Slave*. Mrs. Webb was engaged primarily by anti-slavery lecture series throughout the northern states. When the reading season was over, letters of introduction from Mrs. Stowe to influential anti-slavery supporters helped Mary Webb secure engagements at similar gatherings throughout England.

Mary Webb's physical appearance and vocal qualities were such that she had a pleasing effect on her audiences, one that was startlingly different from the minstrel-inspired characterizations that embodied *Uncle Tom's Cabin* on the commercial stage. H. W. Longfellow described Mrs. Webb as 'this Cleopatra with a white wreath in her dark hair, and a sweet musical voice'.[22] By placing the words of Topsy, Aunt Chloe, Dinah, and Cassy in the mouth of such a reader, who performed without the minstrel signifiers of burnt cork, wild hair, and tattered clothing, Mrs. Stowe eliminated the grotesque comedy that had infiltrated other interpretations of her work.

Though Mrs. Webb presented her readings from a standing position behind a lectern, without benefit of costume, physical action, or scenic embellishment, her ability to capture the attention of her audience is well documented. *The Illustrated London News* describes her performance at the Duchess of Sutherland's house:

Mrs. Webb showed that she possessed considerable and rather peculiar dramatic power. With very little gesticulation and simply by judicious modulations of the voice, combined with earnest and effective delivery, she gave great effect to the last dark, powerful scenes of the drama.[23]

By embodying white, black, men's, and women's voices in a solitary, dignified performance, Mrs. Webb's readings transcended racial prejudice in a manner unusual in pre-Civil War America. Even pro-slavery newspapers commended her performance:

Her rendering of the parts of 'Uncle Tom', 'Little Eva', 'Aunt Chloe', 'Miss Ophelia', 'Marie', and above all 'Topsy' were as nearly natural as it is possible for an imitator to give them. The selections from the drama were in the best of taste and many of the scenes, read in tones varying from the strong and rough to the soft and gentle, from the rushing and boisterous wind to the sighing and musical breeze, were deeply affecting.[24]

The Centrality of Cassy

The effectiveness of Mrs. Webb's performance was enhanced by her gender and racial mirroring of many of the characters in Mrs. Stowe's revised piece. In particular, the audience's identification of Mrs. Webb with the character of Cassy served to create empathy for the desperate plight of the young woman: 'The manner in which Cassy's story was told was especially pathetic; and although, from its length, it threatened to be tedious, the attention of the audience seldom flagged.'[25]

Aware of Mrs. Webb's background from the 'Biographical Sketch' included in the published drama, the reader stood before them as the very incarnation of the play's dramatic heroine. Like the fictional Cassy, Mrs. Webb was a light-skinned, attractive mulatto woman: Cassy's elevated upbringing and education were similar to that of Mrs. Webb; both character and performer were approximately the same age; both had experienced the consequences of an unsanctioned relationship between a slave woman and a white man. In a moment that blurs the distinction between performer and character, Act III opens with Cassy's singing of a love song in Spanish, the language of Mrs. Webb's paternity.

From [Mrs. Webb's] peculiar relation to Christian slaves, she succeeded in commanding the sympathies of her hearers, which she retained to the close of the performance. The various points in the drama were readily appreciated by the audience, and as rapturously applauded as they would be in any theatre in the city.[26]

In addition to her powerful characterization of Cassy, Mrs. Webb achieved dignity in the role of Tom. Unlike the aged, white-haired Uncle Toms to be seen on the popular stage, Mrs. Webb's impersonation brought vitality and vigour to the character. In her representation, the power of youth was restrained only by Uncle Tom's observance of the laws of his faith, and not by fear of earthly retribution.

But Mrs. Webb was most successful in the character of Tom himself. The hoarse negro voice, the solemn tones – those of a man living in a world which seems to be a perpetual contradiction to the laws of that God in whom he firmly believes – were very striking. The piety, the resignation, the humility, and, at the same time, the confidence of Tom's character were brought out fully. The singing of the hymns was remarkably effective. The peculiar negro intonation, the struggle after correctness of melody, the solemn meaning which the singer threw into the words, gave great prominence to this portion of the readings.[27]

Freed by Mrs. Webb's obvious femininity from the audience's stereotyped expectations of appropriate male resistance, Mrs. Webb's 'Tom' retained his dignity despite 'living in a world' that is a 'perpetual con-

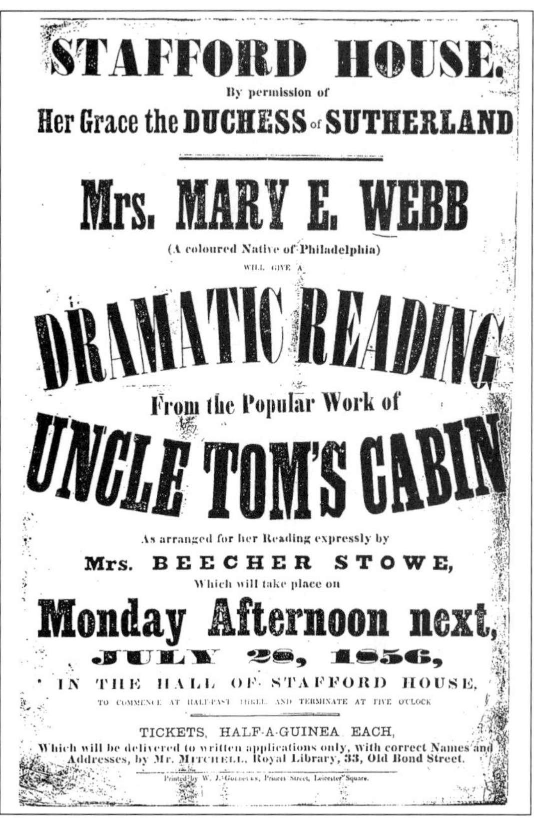

Handbill for Mary Webb's performance at Stafford House (reproduced by courtesy of Harriet Beecher Stowe House, Hartford, Connecticut).

tradiction to the laws of God'. In more ways than one, *The Christian Slave* truly represented the 'resurrection of Uncle Tom'.[28]

Conclusion

The Christian Slave might be better remembered today had its production history not been cut short by Mrs. Webb's death in 1859 at the age of thirty-one. The last reference to a reading of the piece by Mrs. Webb is in Philadelphia in 1857, barely two years after its publication.[29] Following her husband's decision not to stay in the United States, the couple left for Jamaica in 1858, where Frank Webb was appointed to the post office in Kingston. After Mary's death, Mr. Webb married a Jamaican woman, repatriating to the United States in 1869.[30]

Though *The Christian Slave* may have died with Mrs. Webb, her readings may have paved the way for those other young black women who, with Mrs. Stowe's assistance, furthered the anti-slavery cause by appearing throughout the United States and Great Britain. By expanding the lecture forum to include dramatizations of texts in addition to the more standard oratorical devices, Mrs. Webb provided a personalized explication of the horrors of slavery. In a description that might mistakenly be applied to Mrs. Webb, the *National Anti-Slavery Standard* thus reported on a lecture given by another 'particular friend of Mrs. Stowe's', one Miss S. P. Redmond, a 'lady of colour':

She commenced her discourse with all the ease and grace to be expected from an accomplished lady, and the narrative of the wrongs and injustice heaped upon the section of the human family to which she belongs was given with a force and natural truthfulness beyond the reach of art. In all she said, there was something so persuasive, so femininely beautiful and subdued, that made her appear in the estimation of her hearers (though a free woman) one who felt the wrongs and oppressions of her whole tribe, and in her own person endured, through sympathy, their slavery and degradation. . . . She quoted a thrilling passage from a recently published work, describing the sale, by public auction, of a beautiful white woman, yet a slave. . . . [31]

The Christian Slave provided a model that would be incorporated by others attempting to persuade audiences of the indignities and sufferings caused by slavery. The combination of powerful literary quality and fervent emotion, voiced by a reader who represented the most oppressed members of the slavery system, became a powerful weapon in the fight to convert public opinion to the anti-slavery cause. Though Mrs. Stowe would never again write a dramatization of one of her own works, her continued support of women abolitionists speaking in public forums attests to her own positive appraisal of the effects wrought by Mary Webb's performance of *The Christian Slave*.

Notes and References

1. See Forrest Wilson, *Crusader in Crinoline: the Life of Harriet Beecher Stowe* (Lippincott, 1941) and Joan D. Hedrick, *Harriet Beecher Stowe: a Life* (Oxford University Press, 1994).

2. Hedrick, p. 256.

3. *The Illustrated London News*, 2 August 1856, p. 121.

4. Hedrick, p. 249.

5. Mark Akenside, an English poet and physician, published *The Pleasures of Imagination*, a didactic poem, in 1744.

6. *The Liberator*, 26 March 1852.

7. *The Liberator*, 7 July 1852.

8. *The New York Albion*, 7 June 1856.

9. *The New York Herald*, 1 November 1853.

10. Interview with Harriet Beecher Stowe, 1899.

11. Phillip S. Lapsansky, 'Afro-Americana: Frank J. Webb and His Friends', *The Annual Report of the Library Company of Philadelphia for 1990* (Philadelphia, 1991) p. 36.

12. Frank Webb, 'Biographical Sketch', in *The Christian Slave*, by Harriet Beecher Stowe (Phillips, Sampson, and Low, 1856), p. i.

13. 'Biographical Sketch', p. ii.

14. Charlotte Forten Grimke, in Brenda Stevenson, ed., *The Journals of Charlotte Forten Grimke* (Oxford University Press, 1988), p. 144.

15. 'Biographical Sketch', p. ii.

16. Letter from Harriet Beecher Stowe to Mr. and Mrs. Edward Baines, 24 May 1856, Katherine Day Collection, Harriet Beecher Stowe Centre.

17. 'Biographical Sketch', p. iii.

18. Taken from the cast lists found in George Aiken's *Uncle Tom's Cabin; or, Life Among the Lowly*, in Daniel C. Gerould, ed., *American Melodrama* (Performing Arts Journal Publications, 1983), and Harriet Beecher Stowe, *The Christian Slave* (Sampson and Low, 1855), reprinted in Douglas Jerrold, ed., *Jack Runnymede: The Man of Many Thanks* (Bunce and Brother, n.d.).

19. *The Christian Slave* (1855), p. 67.

20. Ibid., p. 58.

21. *The Christian Slave* (Sampson Low, 1856). This rare edition, published to coincide with Mrs. Webb's reading tour of Great Britain, can be found at the Harriet Beecher Stowe House, Hartford, Connecticut.

22. H. W. Longfellow, in Samuel Longfellow, ed., *The Life of H. W. Longfellow, with Extracts from His Journals and Correspondence* (Ticknor, 1886), p. 269.

23. 2 August 1856, p. 122.

24. *The Daily Plain Dealer*, undated clipping, Harriet Beecher Stowe Centre.

25. *The Illustrated London News*, 2 August 1856, p. 122.

26. *Boston Evening Transcript*, 12 December 1855.

27. *The Illustrated London News*, op. cit.

28. *The Worcester Daily Spy*, 8 December 1855.

29. *The Journals of Charlotte Forten Grimke*, p. 264.

30. Jack Selzman, David Lionel Smith, and Cornel West, ed., 'Frank Webb', *Encyclopedia of African-American Culture and History*, Vol. V (Simon and Schuster Macmillan, 1996), p. 2796.

31. *The National Anti-Slavery Standard*, 16 April 1859.

Graham Ley

Theatre of Migration and
the Search for a Multicultural Aesthetic:
Twenty Years of Tara Arts

This year sees the twentieth anniversary of the foremost British-Asian 'company of identity', Tara Arts, directed throughout that time by Jatinder Verma – a major interview with whom forms the core of this celebratory feature. This traces the history and evolving philosophy of the company, from its origins in outrage at a racist murder, through changing perceptions of how multicultural identity can best find its dramatic expression, to a discussion of Verma's own recent work for Contact Theatre and the National. Contributions from other leading participants in the company's work are complemented by a selection of press reactions to major productions, and a survey of bibliographical and other resources. The compiler of this feature, Graham Ley, presently lectures in the Department of Drama at the University of Exeter, having previously taught in London and New Zealand. He is currently completing a book on theatrical theory, on which he has previously also published in NTQ, most recently on 'The Role of Metaphor in Brook's *The Empty Space*' (NTQ35, 1993) and 'The Significance of Diderot' (NTQ44, 1995). Among his publications on ancient performance, *A Short Introduction to the Ancient Greek Theatre* appeared from the University of Chicago Press in 1991.

Jatinder Verma
interviewed by Graham Ley

Evolution of a Company

TARA *presented its first production, Tagore's Sacrifice, in 1977, so this year marks the company's twentieth anniversary. How did it come into being?*

It was, as with most companies, a mixture of accident and intention. The intention part of it relates to 4 June 1976, which was a day when this young Sikh lad in Southall, Gurdeep Singh Chaggar, was killed. It became very obvious within a day or so that this was a racist murder. In retrospect it doesn't seem to be a terribly significant thing, because we've had so many; but at the time it galvanized a particular generation of Asians.

Until then, I suppose, if Asians had an image in the country, it was by and large law-abiding, and certainly non-public. But the events of June 1976 impelled Asians into the public view. Young Asians took to the streets. They made Southall a no-go area, and lots of youth movements developed in many different parts of the country. We were a part of that response. I was at university, and two of those who set up the company with me were studying law. What we'd found was that we'd each reacted in the same way, which was: 'We need to do something.'

Why did you choose theatre as a response?

Well, that's the accident part. When we got together in London, late in 1976, we realized that we shared common interests, and we thought, 'Let's make a film.' But two weeks down that road we realized that none of us knew anything about making films. Moreover, if our intent was to involve a lot of people, then film was not the medium, because only a few of us would be involved in the editing and putting together. But two of us had gone to see an Asian arts event organized by the National Association of Asian Youth at the Royal Albert Hall. I was utterly appalled by the sight of this little girl, seven years old, in a pink frock, with pigtails, who came on to this vast stage at the Royal Albert Hall – and then played Beethoven's *Für Elise*. On the way back in the bus I turned around to my friends and said: 'Listen, I've done a play before, I know of a very good playwright, Tagore. Let's have a look at that. I know of some friends who can help us. At least, between us, I have got a little bit of experience, and it'll involve a lot of people and it'll be *live*. And the things that we are most interested in, which are to raise some sorts of issues, have a discussion, a dialogue with people, will be much more easily achieved with this form.' And that's really how it began.

You are best known at present for your productions of classic European theatre. But what was the policy in the first years, and how did your material reflect that policy? Was there a close relation to the 'language theatre' of the Punjabi, Gujerati, and other communities?

The first thing to remember is that we were very naive in our entry into the theatre – naive in the best sense, in that we really didn't know. We would go round and if there was a play that we liked, and we thought there was something good in it, we would adopt that. That's all we knew: we knew our tastes, if you like. As for a policy, what came out in the first programme note was that we tried to make a link between our relationship with white society and with ourselves. In short, there is a link between racism at one end of the spectrum of oppression, injustice, and discrimination, and things that might be going on within our own community, which could be relations between parents and children, or relations between different religious communities.

If we only focused on racism we would die, because we would have to make the assumption that 'we are better than them', and that's a false assumption to make. So we need to be as critical of ourselves as we are of the society outside, and I think that has

been the saving grace of the company. I do not think we would have survived for twenty years, and developed in the way we have, had we not had that almost instinctive sense of our political aims, and set it out.

How were those aims reflected in the early scripts?

Even though the plays in the early period were all scripted, devised, or written by me, and were original, it would be false to say they were completely contemporary. A lot of them dialogued with history, particularly the Raj. Often we would mix up a situation that happened in the Raj with an event that happened in our own time. So while the plays were looking critically at the workings of the Raj or at teachers in a school, at the structures of white society, they were also, no less critically, looking at some practices in Asian society that were not at all wonderful, for want of a better word.

That meant we were placed in ambivalent territory. On the one hand, there was a recognition, almost a claiming of us by our own community: 'Someone is out there on the public stage, doing things about us!' And on the other hand, there was a certain distance from the community, because we were also quite prepared to be critical, and not just give the community what it wanted. I think that's been a feature of the company right through.

By the early 'eighties we also began to realize that something was awry. I suppose the first realization was that if theatre was what we wanted to do, then we had to be cognizant of the rules of the game. What could be better done as a speech, even a political speech, should be done as a political speech: theatre demands other things – looking at structures, at plots, starting to think about metaphors.

Your language of communicating was English?

Yes. That was a conscious decision in 1977, with the first play. And our reasoning was that even if we were concerned only to attract an Asian audience – which we weren't, but even if we were – then which Asian audience? Which Indian language? If we spoke in Hindi, the Bengalis would be left out; if we spoke in Bengali, then the Gujeratis and the Punjabis would be left out. The corollary was that the English that we choose to work in had to be *our* English, inflected by our concerns and our languages and our kind of idiom.

But that remained a theoretical statement for the first four or five years. There was an extraordinary disjunction then between the language we employed in rehearsal, where a lot of us modulated between English, Punjabi, Gujerati, and our actual work in front of the audience, which was entirely in English, even to the point where we were caricaturing ourselves: when we had Indian characters they spoke a broken English. We never allowed ourselves to speak our own language.

But then we realized we were lying to ourselves. Our reality is that we negotiate several languages, but we are not putting that reality on to the stage. Sure, if we are true to ourselves, then we have a problem: what about the audience that doesn't understand that odd word or phrase or sentence in Hindi or in Punjabi or in whatever other language? Well, that's a theatrical problem: you have to find other means through which people can understand. And that was a huge, huge breakthrough.

Tara became a professional touring company in 1982 with Lion's Raj, *directed by Tony Clark. How had that decision been arrived at, and what was your intention in touring?*

What's important to bear in mind is that from the beginning, from 1978, we had had outside directors: we didn't know, so we decided to get the expertise in. The first person was Gerald Chapman, from the Royal Court's Young People's Theatre, and he directed two of our shows. We were very clear what we wanted, and that was the tools of the craft. So the people who came in were aware that they were coming for a specific purpose, and for a limited period of time. It might last a project, it might last two

<table>
<tr><td colspan="2">Selected Productions by Tara Arts</td></tr>
<tr><td>1977</td><td>Sacrifice</td></tr>
<tr><td>1980</td><td>Inkalaab 1919</td></tr>
<tr><td>1982</td><td>Lion's Raj</td></tr>
<tr><td>1984</td><td>Chilli in Your Eyes</td></tr>
<tr><td>1985</td><td>Miti ki gadi (The Little Clay Cart)</td></tr>
<tr><td></td><td>Anklets of Fire</td></tr>
<tr><td></td><td>This Story Is Not for Telling</td></tr>
<tr><td>1986</td><td>The Little Clay Cart</td></tr>
<tr><td></td><td>The Broken Thigh</td></tr>
<tr><td></td><td>Tejo Vanio</td></tr>
<tr><td>1987</td><td>Exile in the Forest</td></tr>
<tr><td></td><td>Bicharo</td></tr>
<tr><td>1988</td><td>Bhavni Bhavai</td></tr>
<tr><td>1989</td><td>Danton's Death</td></tr>
<tr><td>1990</td><td>Tartuffe</td></tr>
<tr><td></td><td>The Emperor and the Beggar</td></tr>
<tr><td></td><td>The Proposal</td></tr>
<tr><td></td><td>The Government Inspector</td></tr>
<tr><td>1991</td><td>Oedipus the King</td></tr>
<tr><td></td><td>Heer Ranjha</td></tr>
<tr><td></td><td>The Little Clay Cart</td></tr>
<tr><td>1992</td><td>Heer and Romeo</td></tr>
<tr><td>1993</td><td>Troilus and Cressida</td></tr>
<tr><td>1994</td><td>The Mufti from Istanbul</td></tr>
<tr><td></td><td>Le Bourgeois Gentilhomme</td></tr>
<tr><td>1995</td><td>Cyrano</td></tr>
<tr><td>1997</td><td>A Midsummer Night's Dream</td></tr>
</table>

projects. In 1982, in fact, we had two people, Tony Clark and David Sulkin, who directed the community show.

Professional status came about organically. Up to 1982 we were mounting three productions a year – touring them outside London at the weekends while working in London during the week. So we were working professionally, with people rehearsing, in some cases, five nights a week. By 1982 it had become clear that there were some individuals who really had committed everything to this, and for them the logical thing seemed to be to do it full time, to get paid for it. That's really how that shift occurred. But having made that shift, I think it had a logic of its own, which did result in the community aspect of the company going into the background.

Tara's work in the 1980s seems to me to be characterized by an increasing ambition to develop a distinctive theatrical style. Is that fair?

At the heart of the 1980s was this increasing feeling that the manner in which we were presenting our work was alienating: the work was in English, without reference to our own languages, was in a fringe mode, while the audiences were reflections of ourselves. We never had the range, either in terms of age, or in terms of races, and that's what troubled us. What made the company distinct? Was it just the presence of dark-skinned actors on stage, and a particular kind of material? We began to feel that it must also be about the manner of presentation, about the aesthetics.

In 1981 a company from Pune in India came to the Riverside Studios in London with a production called *Gashiram Kotwal*, which was directed by Jabbar Patel. Now what was extraordinary about that was that this was a play in Marathi, a language which none of us understood. But it was totally comprehensible, because it was what is considered in the West an excellent example of total theatre – music, movement, and speech formed the production text. There was no set: the set consisted of a wall which was a chorus. That really opened our eyes to the need for us to have that kind of distinctive dramaturgy, and put us on the road to developing an aesthetic which was premised on Indian theatre.

Then in 1984 I did *The Little Clay Cart*, an eighth-century Sanskrit play. Doing that production we had our first encounter with the *Natyasastra*, the treatise on the aesthetics of Indian theatre which has informed all Indian performing arts over the last two thousand years. What began then to emerge was a sense of qualities of text, of text that could handle that kind of epic approach. But the texts we were producing ourselves were simply not good enough, so it became a deliberate attempt to encounter other texts.

With the opening of the Earlsfield, London, centre in 1985 Tara was able to establish a theatre-in-education company, which was closed in 1989. Could you describe the activities and role of that company during those years?

Our understanding was that any company like this had got an educative role within the framework of British theatre, and indeed of Britain. When we started we were the only one, and even now we remain one of only a few, and we constantly felt the pressure of people coming to see our shows in order to find out more about Asian culture. But there was a limited extent to which we could ever satisfy that particular need: a production is a production, and it has its own particular dynamic. So we began to think that we should try and fulfil that need by specifically intervening, and that's how we set about the formation of the TIE company.

After four years it folded, or rather we closed it – but that really had to do less with financial pressures than with two other concerns. One was that it was impossible to transfer casts, to have the same body of people now working in a different guise with the TIE company. So what was happening was that we would have two separate companies out on the road at the same time, and it was really impossible to give the same level of commitment and passion to both. The other thing, which was very serious, was that after four years of working – and these were secondary schools we were going into, working with thirteen- to sixteen-year-olds – it was obvious that we were acting as a kind of sticking-plaster for the school's own problems. In a lot of cases there were clearly racial and cultural tensions, which we became the sop for when there was no context for it in the school itself. Those two sets of pressures made it necessary to close the company.

Stylistically, it is very clear that in 1985 the influence of Anuradha Kapur, an expert in folk drama from Delhi, became decisive. Could you describe what Kapur brought to Tara, and how it has affected a continuing sense of mise-en-scène?

Anuradha Kapur has undoubtedly been an extraordinarily critical influence, and continues as a kind of collaborator. There were several things that she made us aware of. One was a different kind of notion of modernity: here was an Indian woman who had specialized in what is regarded as folk

'The Little Clay Cart'

Jatinder Verma is the brainiest of all multi-cultural theatre spokesmen in Britain, but his work on the stage does not always match the quality of his polemicism. No complaints, though, about *The Little Clay Cart*. . . . Here, the Indian deities humorously supervise the love of a Brahmin merchant for a rich courtesan threatened by the intervention of the blustery brother of a bad king. The story is enmeshed in the fascinating metaphor of the rolling dice and an appealing, trance-like style of performance which Verma relates in his programme to *rasa* theory, 'the evocation of the state of rapture through aesthetic distance'.

Michael Coveney, *The Observer*

Imagine a blend of Christmas pantomime and Greek tragedy, with Irish jokes and movement to stop Marcel Marceau dead in his tracks, and you will have some idea of Jatinder Verma's multi-national production of *The Little Clay Cart*. Verma and his co-adapter, Ranjit Bolt, have gone all out to meet the English spectator half way with this Sanskrit masterpiece. You may have trouble sizing up the situation and characters (this evidently not being a priority in eighth-century India); but once the basic elements – two lovers persecuted by a royal tyrant – are grasped, what follows is stage poetry of a high order.

Irving Wardle, *Independent on Sunday*

I feared an inaccessible museum piece, but Jatinder Verma's English version of the Sanskrit original (with additional verse and songs by the ubiquitous Ranjit Bolt) turns out to be wonderfully fresh and inviting. . . . The sheer high spirits of the piece render all resistance futile. The lively, disputatious dialogue, crammed with proverbs and elaborate similes, has an engaging vitality, and Verma's exuberant production also features singing, dancing, and hypnotic original Indian music by V. Chandran played on a wide variety of instruments by two on-stage musicians.

Charles Spencer, *Daily Telegraph*

The obvious danger is of embalming the whole thing in a remote folksy exoticism. Mr. Verma avoids that by making it clear we are watching a classic play presented by modern Asian and Irish actors who slip in jokes about takeaways and who squat on benches in Magdalen Rubalcava's three-tiered, crimson-boarded, temple-like set. . . . Mr. Verma has a great talent for picking physically attractive performers and, even more important, for re-animating a Sanskrit classic such as this to uncover its core of genuine democratic gaiety.

Michael Billington, *The Guardian*

The fairy-tale beauty of the piece is much enhanced by Magdalen Rubalcava's lovely set – a red platform-like structure backed by Indian wall-paintings, and a planked floor with trap-doors which open up to reveal little enticing pools of lotus blossom. Performed by a cast composed of Indian and Irish actors (which results in some hilarious collisions of tone), the proceedings are interspersed with stamping Indian dances and an exercise that looks like an oriental version of the Highland Fling. . . . There is much in *The Little Clay Cart* that might have been grist to Brecht's mill and there is, in fact, a Brechtian tinge to the couple of songs Ranjit Bolt has contributed.

Paul Taylor, *The Independent*

theatre, but is essentially popular theatre, and who was constantly assaulting your own notion of the modern in herself. She represented in her own thinking the kind of journey we were going through – the realization there is not a separation between the contemporary and the historical or traditional, between our present as migrants here and a past that is fitfully remembered, but that there is a negotiation, a dialogue.

The other thing that she brought lay in terms of technique. I feel that she is the best director that I've ever come across in terms of devising, with an absolutely meticulous approach. To see a text emerge out of nothing was extraordinarily stimulating, and it set up several trains of thought. So for me those were the two things, particularly that very acute notion of the modern – that it is not premised on Fukuyama's phrase 'the end of history', but is modern precisely because it maintains a critical dialogue with the pre-modern.

A second, significant influence was the visit in 1987 by Professor Sankara Pillai from Kerala, who brought skills in the martial art Kalari, which affected the physicality of Exile in the Forest *that same year.*

What came through with Sankara Pillai was a slight variant on Anuradha. Here was a person who was steeped in all the traditions of the performing arts in his part of India – which is Kerala, in south-west India – but who had a refreshing approach to them. He was undertaking this project of documenting every single traditional performing arts activity in his state, and his sense was that 'I'm not interested in keeping these forms alive, that's not why I'm doing it. Forms are like humans, they are born, they have a period of activity, of life, and they die, and they ought to die. That's not to be mourned. What is useful and necessary is to know how they worked, what were their dramaturgical principles, what were their techniques, so that these might inspire others after them.'

Around him was a set of performers, some from Kalari the martial art, and some who were modern performers. What was very interesting about Kalari was to see the vital relationship in Kerala itself between this martial arts form, which is a couple of millennia old, and the performing arts. In fact, one was the origin of the other: the relationship with the ground, the relationship of the body to the floor, really stemmed from Kalari.

I think the greatest legacy of Sankara Pillai, who unfortunately died in 1989, is that the performers who came with him and became a part of our company have brought not only distinctive techniques but also a distinctive imagination into successive productions. I certainly see them as part of my core company.

The medieval Gujerati form of folk drama, Bhavai, has also been a significant constituent of Tara's repertoire, with such productions as Tejo Vanio, Zanda Zulam, Bicharo, Bhavni Bhavai, *and* Tartuffe. *Could you describe how Bhavai has contributed to the aesthetics practised by Tara?*

Bhavai is really commedia dell'arte – that is, its very close equivalent in the West is the commedia. It's from the same period, and some Italian theatre anthropologists have even suggested that there might be another kind of link: that the face-masks of Bhavai could even have led to the masks used in commedia. It shares all the same features. In commedia one has the *lazzi*: there is a basic situation, and the rest is improvisation, done by the company of actors responding to their times and to their audiences. Bhavai has absolutely the same thing, with the *vesh* as the basic plot-line. This is embellished by a group of specialist performers: there is the fool, there is the equivalent of Arlecchino (*Rangla*), all the kinds of stock characters are there, and they respond to whatever locality they happen to be in. There is movement and there is music, and there is this extraordinary 'text'.

For me there were two things about Bhavai. One was that up to the time that we began encountering Bhavai – and in a sense Anuradha provided the bridge – our notion of Indian theatre was very much informed by the classics. While I had an appreciation that even within the dramaturgy as laid out by the *Natyasastra* there was this distinction between *natya*, which is a kind of stylized drama, and *lokya*, which is of the people, I hadn't really had any encounter with *lokya*. Here was a form which was intact, which had no classical status at all, which was literally of the people, and yet which shared many of the features that we had begun to explore as a result of working on the classics, though its movement patterns were not as strict or as defined as they were in the classics.

I think the key sensibility which informs Bhavai – and informed us – was irreverence. Bhavai has got to take liberties with its audiences, with its times, but it has to do it in a manner which is not alienating or offensive. So there is a kind of cheekiness about it. Those were the features which became like finding honey.

Tara has performed classics from the Sanskrit tradition, specifically Bhasa's The Broken Thigh *and Shudraka's* The Little Clay Cart. *Do you see these inclusions as essential, as theatrically evangelical, or simply as some amongst many choices for Tara?*

I think the Indian classics are all those three things for us. They are essential; they are deliberate, strategic choices; and they just happen to be part of the repertoire of great works. To take the essential: the migrant, the outsider works on the peculiar axis of memory and present. For us as a company, if we do not have a dialogue with our past, part of which is the classical Sanskrit tradition, then we are only partially having a vital dialogue, only partially being modern.

In the same way, if we did not have a dialogue with Shakespeare, with Gogol, with Chekhov, people today would consider that to be only a partial sense of the 'modern'. This returns to what I felt about Anuradha, that to be modern is to have this kind of dialogue. For the Asian actor that becomes even more fraught, because of this vexed question of identity. There is an increasing

sense in me now that part of the migrant condition in English society is to be a tourist of your own body. In some senses the act of us looking at India or China, with us being in England and part of English society, is to be tourists, because we're not part of those societies. It's the act of looking at the other.

How one gets influenced by the other is a different thing. The peculiarity for the migrant is that in a way all those acts then become also a way of looking into your own self, and in that sense being a tourist of your own body. Because part of your body, part of your blood, part of your memory is actually of that landscape. And I find that condition a very interesting one, because it opens up two sorts of strands: tourism as consumption, as commodity, but tourism also as provocation.

Personally I think that what Tara has manifested so far, and certainly what keeps me ticking, is the latter – tourism as provocation. There lies the distinction between the act of a company like us encountering India and other parts of Asia, Japan, or China, and a company like Mnouchkine's, or Brook's, encountering those cultures. I don't think the provocation, the provoking of one's own sense of what one is, is inherent in those projects, but I think it is inherent in ours.

Could you talk about the significance of musical performance in Tara's work: influences, skills, practitioners?

As we began to become conscious of a dramaturgy that was not a modern European dramaturgy we began to realize that music plays a very critical part. Music is not ancillary, it's not atmosphere: it is text, which is the equivalent of speech. That was a route into working much more formally with music and musicians. There has been a whole variety of musicians – Srivestava, Adrian Lee, Chandran – and for me it is Chandran who has acted as a sort of template, a guide to what is the ideal musician for theatre.

He was one of the performers who came with Sankara Pillai – classically trained in Carnatic music, fully conversant with Hindustani music, but someone who has an intuitive sense that theatre, unlike music, is not a pure medium. It is founded on impurity, on actually bending the rules: it's a bastard form, in other words. And the ability he has is to create the theatrical moment musically, which may not be the musical moment. It may even be musically impure, because the *ragas* he is using may not be one *raga* at all, but go from one *raga* into another, or there may be a folk song that turns into a *raga*.

The more I've worked with him, the more I've recognized two things. Firstly, while I admire the energy, the dynamism, the wit, and the creativity of modern music, I always have a sense – I sense it in the cities in England – that it is a music that has no organic relationship with life. You hear music in your ear, in cars, on radios, on television, you buy it and listen to it, but as you walk down the street you don't hear music in the bodies of the people, you don't see the people suddenly bursting into song. And so I recognized that when music is used in the theatre it must be used because there is this organic relationship, because there is an effect on the body, an effect on the voice. That was one thing that Chandran released.

The other was the recognition of the problems of achieving that organic relationship, when the tools I had were actually quite limited. I think modern actors in England, irrespective of whether they are Asian or not, and perhaps more problematically if they are Asian, have no music, or that their universe of music is very narrow. It's reflected in the body, since the body doesn't suggest a dance; it's reflected in the rhythm, since the notion of rhythm is quite restricted, a basic four-beat one; and it's reflected in the imagination, in the notion that acting is not singing, and singing is not acting. That's what I mean by the inorganic nature of our experience of music.

So far I have tried to impose this sense of an organic music; but now I am more acutely aware that I have got to find that relationship the other way round – to take people with their current or modern English sense of music, with all its fragmentation, with all its alienation, and to use that fragmentation to get to an organic relationship. If the four-beat is the only thing that makes sense, then let's try and make sense of the four-beat.

This has a particular relationship to Asian actors, because I began to realize very early on that, for Asians who were born here, Indian music was as alien as for any other English person. But for the Asian actor an encounter with Indian music had to surmount barriers of identity: 'Do I want to be associated with being Indian? This is all from the past, this is all traditional, but I want to be like everyone else.' For the English actor there is no such problem: there is simply the response that, 'This is quite a cool thing', or 'This is a new thing, and I want to work with it.' Those are the kind of challenges I see in terms of music.

Much is said and written of the impact of Theatre de Complicite, whose physical skills owe, it seems, a great deal to Le Coq. The Indian performance tradition is implicitly one of integrated text and movement. How have you determined an appropriate physicality for Tara's work?

Our movement sensibility has stemmed from two sources. One is the recognition of the power of music in my own imagination: for me this has been Indian music, and invariably that has meant the classical vocal tradition. In a sense the notion of movement for me comes from that. The second, social source clearly has been Shobana Jeyasingh. Of critical importance was our early appreciation of the fundamental relationship in all classical Indian dance between the pure dance aspect and what's called *abhinaya*, which is expressive dance. Every dancer has to be proficient in both – pure dance being about patterns, rhythms, the body-in-space, with no meaning, with no story attached, *abhinaya* being the body-as-actor, who is creating a very particular world, and depicts a very particular story, and therefore the body-as-text.

It was the *abhinaya* aspect which became our own route into movement; but I became aware early that I was dealing with bodies which don't, when they stand at the bus-stop, naturally make a gesture, as I have seen bodies do in India. So I've become conscious that I need to take the principle of *abhinaya* from the actors' bodies. I think now in the same way I am thinking of music, that if one needs to start with their present notion of what is music, then the same has to occur with the body. So the *abhinaya* – the gestural language, the mimetic, expressive language in terms of the story – has to come from the way in which they use their bodies to express themselves now.

Now if that has to mean that there are influences of body-popping, or of the disco, or of acrobatics, well, that's fine. I feel that what we need to do now is to take in those influences and formalize them, and therefore build up a distinctive *abhinaya* which is not quite mine, but which is made by the actors carving text quite consciously and intuitively from their own bodies. So I have begun to release myself from a more formal approach, and now if I call in Shobana it's for something specific, or it is to come and have a look at a choreography; when I began she would have been there right at the beginning, to lay out the choreography.

But partly because of Shobana, and of my own training from her, my eye is sometimes very resistant to the informality of the body, and the thing that I find most awkward is that the modern body has no expression of the hand. The curvature of the hand, the tactility of the hand, is simply not there. In India part of the tactility comes because one eats with the hands as one does a lot of other work with the hands. Here there is a sense in which the hand is alien.

Those are things I am becoming more and more conscious of: if that's the nature of the hand, how can one make this ungainly item of the modern body look quite eloquent on the stage? The body must be eloquent and specific in the way in which the word is specific.

You started with Tagore's Sacrifice, *which is a protest against a violent religiosity and an allegory in favour of pacifism under colonial rule. Your first adaptation of a European classic,* The Government Inspector, *offered an ironic vision of colonialism. Are your motives for staging classics consistently political?*

I think they are political in the sense that I am conscious as a person that life is political. There's been a kind of mistake in recent English theatre history in the distinction betwen agit-prop and 'real' theatre: I think all theatre is inherently political, because you make choices. You choose to work with this particular cast as opposed to that particular cast, you choose to play a particular text at a particular moment in time: and those choices are related to your sense of your society at any given moment. That's the general position.

The only thing I would add is that the very inception of Tara was a conscious political move – a reaction to a murder and to the crying need to achieve public presence in the condition of a relative absence in English society. And I think that's a peculiarity of the Asian migrant, and even of the non-migrant Asian in this country, that we exist in a kind of 'present absence' or have an 'absent presence'. The absence of us in the normality, the everydayness of life, is all too apparent: whether it's on television or radio, in newspapers or in education, there is an all-pervasive absence.

But for me the real heart of it lies in the fact that we are not present in the imagination – in the imagination of white writers or in the imagination of English people, although English people are present in our imagination. And that's what the politics really are, that's the political condition.

In this respect, you have to my mind a stronger insistence on history than many theatre directors. This influenced early work by Tara on the Inkalaab *massacre of 1919, on Gandhi, and on the lives of Asians in Britain before the 1960s. Is it likely to remain as strong?*

Absolutely. James Baldwin, in that extraordinary novel-cum-short story *The Fire Next Time*, says this: 'Know your history well. The purpose of history is not to drown in the past, but it is to go forward.' I've always been fascinated by history, but when I came across that sentence I thought it completely fitted in with the condition of being a migrant. To some extent the whole course of my life is to try and seam up the cracks in the mirror of our experience. And I don't think it's ever possible. The most that would be possible is that I become aware of each fragment.

Now, in that, history is absolutely critical, because it gives you a sense that you are part of a stream of life. I don't think that is a demeaning of oneself, or a loss of one's own individuality: it is actually an acceptance that one exists in a stream of work. I have a particular contribution in this particular moment in time, but I am not the origin of it.

I am not the end of it. That's as important to me in the theatre as it is to any individual who lives. One needs the sense that one has a past, a link – that one hasn't just come from nowhere.

The modern exists because of its negotiations with the past, and in those negotiations several possible futures come up and take on a shape: they don't dictate to the future, but they open up possibilities of what could be your next move. That's where I continue to feel that the most important training for any director would be not theatre but history.

The theme of exile was treated very differently in Exile in the Forest, *in which the exile of the Pandavas and their confusion is an allegory for the state of Asians in the contemporary 'jungle of the cities', and in the more symbolic confusions of performers representing Sophocles'* Oedipus, *seen as a symbolic exile.*

Exile in the Forest was a more straightforward allegory, and its source was in the *Mahabharata*, where there is this section where the heroes – to use a simplistic term – are exiled in the forest for thirteen years. That is part of the grand myths of all cultures: the rites of passage, the forest as the necessary condition for self-knowledge, for a coming-to-terms with who one is, and a preparation for the tribulations of life that have yet to come.

In 1986-87 I had the sense that, by the act of translation into England, we had come into the forest, in that it is unknown, it is weird, there are new rules of the game to learn, and there are pitfalls. There are also some joyous adventures, but all of it is a crucible in which you discover who you are and what you are. The problem with that allegory was what comes after: I didn't have a solution at the time, and to some extent I don't have a solution now, except perhaps a greater sense that the only solution is what you create in the worlds of fantasy: that's in your power, the act of the imagination.

So you can, if you like, reinvent the whole territory as you think it should be, because at the moment one can't say what is the shape of England to come. We are still in that kind of crucible, amplified vastly by the critical identity question that the whole country is faced with, as a result of Europe. There is an historical irony here: England is going through now what we all went through as a result of colonialism. 'Who am I? How do I exert myself?'

In *Oedipus* I felt that – having just done the first production at the National, *Tartuffe*, and it proving to be a success – if I wasn't careful then the head would swell and I would fall. Pride, overweening pride. The sense I had in *Oedipus* was of the *hubris* of the migrant who has made good, who has achieved every single dream of the migrant, to be 'boss'. After all, he had achieved more than any real migrant ever will: he ends up as the ruler of a foreign country, and he marries the queen. What greater fantasy can you have? With that came pride, that overweening pride that I am the creator of it all, by my efforts it has happened, that I am great.

That was my sense with *Oedipus*, but in some ways it shared a vein that has been there for quite a while, and that was best articulated with *The Government Inspector*, where we'd turned the whole mirror onto ourselves, poking fun at ourselves – this ability to turn the barbs on ourselves, and say 'watch it'.

There have inevitably been problems – critical or practical – as well as successes. My impression is that both Troilus and Cressida, *with Contact Theatre, Manchester, and* Cyrano, *with the National Theatre, caused problems. . . .*

I think the problem with *Troilus* was that I flew too much against the nature of the text. The text is fragmentary in nature. But the picture I presented of the world of *Troilus and Cressida* was itself incoherent and fragmented, and that's too much. The audience needs to have some kind of *locus* of coherence from which to make the journey into the incoherence of this work. That was a big tactical error, a real failing to recognize how we travel into story, a kind of deliberate defiance of a basic human need, which is for

The Government Inspector (1990).

'Troilus and Cressida'

At its opening in Manchester recently, this production was greeted by critics with a resounding raspberry. Director Jatinder Verma was pronounced guilty of muddling the play with references to race and war and of cutting some of the play's best-known speeches. More power to his elbow, I say. Anyone looking for an uninterrupted reading of Shakespeare's allegedly original text (which in fact survives in two different versions, printed in a hurry) should stay at home and read it.

Tom Morris

This is a difficult play, both thematically and technically: with its profusion of talkative characters and its odd construction, it is always a challenge to the audience. This production does not do enough to ease the difficulties. The story is simply not told clearly enough. . . . Demandingly against the liberal grain, the approach to the text is fascinating; but especially for the young audiences Contact aims at, it is vital that the basic narrative should be equally absorbing.

Jeffrey Wainwright, *The Independent*

It seems as if we are in for a highly charged political reading of Shakespeare's embittered masterpiece. What we actually get is a formal, stylized, heavily cut, and visually powerful lamentation for a fallen world. Seven actors, of mixed Asiatic, French, and Anglo-Chinese origin, play multiple roles and even swap genders (Cressida and Helen are played by a man, Thersites and Diomedes by a woman) on a stage encircled by tiny, terracotta props, mirrors and drums, pipes and cymbals. If anything, the production seems informed by elegiac pain rather than political urgency.

Michael Billington, *The Guardian*

There is some powerfully truthful acting once the plot is allowed to engage, and brilliantly extended sequences of fire and mirror imagery, which increase the impact of the prophetic and battlefield scenes by converting them into spectacles of ritual beauty. Here, and in its use of music (singing voices combining with textual lamentation), the production presents a compelling argument for multicultural Shakespeare. Eventually, if not quite yet, the club will have to find room for it.

Irving Wardle, *Independent on Sunday*

'A Midsummer Night's Dream'

Much of it is a mess; much of it is the kind of mess that any misguided company could have come up with nowadays. There is nothing particularly multi-racial about putting Bottom on roller-skates, or getting Oberon and Puck to blow bubbles during the lovers' quarrel, or sitting actors with their backs to the stage, or skipping around in circles while delivering a major speech. Some of the magic survives, even so. Odd fragments of the poetry float around.

John Gross, *Sunday Telegraph*

The real test of any Shakespeare production is whether it makes you listen to the verse afresh: here I found it did. When Lysander harshly cried to Hermia: 'Get you gone, you dwarf, you minimus of hindering knot-grass made', the audience roared with outraged laughter. Contrast Robert Lepage's production at the National, where these lines were lost because the actors were squelching in mud, or Miller's, where they were delivered with a weary lassitude. Mr. Verma's version is not only full of primary colours, visual invention, and pleasingly varied accents: it also achieves its effects through the language, which is why it deserves something better than lofty put-downs.

Michael Billington, *Country Life*

You would have thought that this of all plays, exploring the secret affinities between dreams, plays, and passions, would have benefited from eastern theatre; but no, all you get is a certain amount of stylized movement, Indian and Indian-sounding music, and a suggestion of oriental styles in the clothes. That is not a new reading, only a new look.

John Peter, *Sunday Times*

As you would expect, this production has a truly global vision. The multi-ethnic cast employs classical Indian rhythms, Japanese dance, New York rap, a myriad of accents, languages, and songs to create its own version of Shakespeare's enchanted forest. . . . Shakespeare's genius is that he is always open to varying interpretations. Tara's abiding strength has been its insistence on seeing the familiar through new cultural eyes. It is a good marriage and a timely reminder that high art is not the privilege of the European RADA-trained few.

Meera Syal, *The Express*

---

a linear narrative. I think that this need is severely problematic, but so far I'm convinced that nothing has really shaken it.

For me the best example is provided by the two very different narratives, or narrators, Salman Rushdie's *The Moor's Last Sigh*,

From the Tara Arts production of *A Midsummer Night's Dream*, directed by Jatinder Verma (1997), with Pauline Black as Titania and Nizwar Karanj as Bottom.

as opposed to Vikram Seth's *A Suitable Boy*. Both have been critical successes, but *A Suitable Boy* has been an enormous commercial success, and a lot of that has been due to the fact that Vikram Seth provides a coherent narrative. In *The Moor's Last Sigh* you start by thinking this is India, and then suddenly it's Spain, or Europe – a deliberate breaking of the linear narrative, which is why Salman Rushdie is so difficult a writer for many people to consume. With Vikram, you know the dish that you're having; with Salman, you can begin to consume it, but you'll be pretty well guaranteed to have a stomach-ache or a headache fairly soon, because of the nature of the narrative. And that's his reflection of what it means to be modern, what it means to be a migrant.

I think *Troilus* manifested that problem. With *Cyrano* I think that the problem was fundamentally one of post-colonial culture. We had an actor who is the equivalent of any good actor anywhere, but who was coming from a world which was not just Indian cinema, but which had a particular attitude to England as the repository of the greatness of theatre. Yet he was going to be working with a company whose entire history was founded on a questioning of this assumption. That's where the marriage was bound to end in divorce, and that's exactly what happened.

With A Midsummer Night's Dream, *in conjunction with the Lyric Theatre, Hammersmith, Tara will be celebrating twenty years of life.*

Should the critics have expected a political edge to this as well?

The most crucial thing for me is the look of the company. It is a deliberate act, to make overt what I think has been the covert agenda of Tara for the past twenty years, right from the time of *Sacrifice*. Covertly, what we have been about has been a kind of cross-culturalism, a multiculturalism, an encounter of cultures. Why I say 'covertly' is because Tara seemed to the public to be all Asian, or basically Indian – while we have always been aware that what that masked was our enormous cultural variety. So there were actors who were born and bred here who had no knowledge of any Indian languages, nor of India, nor of any Indian literature. There were also actors who were born in India, whose first language was an Indian language, whose imaginative space was Indian. And there were actors who were not from India, nor from here, but from another part of the world.

So there was this variety, and as we continued to do work we were constantly negotiating between those cultures. Last year it began to hit me more and more that the public perception of the company is of an Indian company, and that that perception needs to be challenged. Also, our funding history has been as an Asian company, and perhaps this needs to be challenged. So with the *Dream* there is a huge and also obvious variety of cast – from an English actress to a Nigerian-English actress, to a Burmese, to a Chinese, to an Afro-Caribbean, to an Indian.

I don't know what the consequence of that is going to be. Some of the the ground has been cut from under the feet of a lot of people, and I'm not necessarily sure that's a good thing. Within our own community of performers, there's a sense of 'What's Tara now? In what sense is it Asian?' And from another sector of the community, and from a lot of the critics, comes a preference for the kind of coherent narrative we were presenting before, which was a world which was distinctively Indian in one sense or another.

Now I think that that's partly their problem, because it's part of the incoherence of modern England. But I knew before I was going to do the *Dream*, and I had signalled it, that the *Dream* would be my last European text for three years: that's how I was going to mark the end of the twenty years, and the beginning of the next twenty years. Which is not to say it would be the last time ever that Tara would look at Shakespeare. But for the next three years I want to look at other texts, those which are regarded as 'other', be they from India, China, Japan, or Africa. But definitely not from Europe.

Could you describe how the company works on a production? Is there a characteristic process?

There isn't a process that covers all the productions, for obvious reasons: each text is different. There is a feature, which is a certain kind of ritualizing of the rehearsal process: we begin with this exercise, which is the sun prayer – a yoga-based exercise, which I feel is a good flexing of the body. Increasingly I am also using that, or another variant, to close the rehearsal: so we come from whatever crap of the day and we induct ourselves into the work of the day, and then let go of the work of the day, and go off and do whatever each one wants.

Beyond that the characteristic is a certain kind of space: between the director and the text, space for the actor to find the text and kick it around a little bit before it begins to achieve a tighter focus or gets set. What this characteristic is leading to is the joy of performance, some little idiosyncrasy that the actor has. I don't think that comes without this bit of playing around.

Having said that, I know I am becoming more hooked on text. You read in the space, you move: but you read and read and read, which means in effect you're acting all the time. I'm then getting some sense of what the mise-en-scène will be, what could be the choreography and the possible interpretation. That's happening with certain types of project, of course: with *A Midsummer Night's Dream* it was essential. They moved, they were on the set, they explored while they were reading. And then they could stop the reading. Either they could stop it, or the

From the Tara Arts production of *Troilus and Cressida*, directed by Jatinder Verma (1993), with Vincent Ebrahim as Hector (left) and Nirmal Chandra Pandey as Ajax.

listener could stop it, if I didn't understand a word or a phrase, or I didn't quite get what the point was from a particular line. Interrupt, open out a discussion, and carry on.

I found that a very good way of refining the particular dramaturgy for that project. In the case of *Bottom's Dream*, the children's version of the *Dream* which I've just finished, it's different because the text is a resource, and only a resource. We knew that we could not do the entire text of Shakespeare's *A Midsummer Night's Dream* in front of seven- to ten-year-olds, so it had to be compressed. I wanted them to experience the language, but much of that language is way above the vocabulary of seven- to ten-year-olds. So we set up a mode where that text sits with our own inventive text, and what we came up with was rhyming couplets, which the actors constructed, of the story of the *Dream*.

And for the main house, there were specific workshops. Is that standard practice?

So far the characteristic has been to do workshops in other forms as part of rehearsals. With the *Dream*, for the first time, I did those workshops a month before the rehearsals started. There were two reasons. Firstly I realized there was too much of a weight on actors in rehearsals to encounter other forms, and often one saw the results of that by the end of the tour. Secondly, I wanted to avoid imposing form, and to give the actors the space to let the form come through their imagination and their experience. That's why it was necessary to do the workshops a month before, and that's something I'll retain for subsequent productions. It also sets up a common language straight away, and that's one of the reasons why the rehearsals were some of the best I've had, because they came with a shared language.

For the *Dream* there were also particular things I was interested in – Beijing Opera, West African dance, Morris dancing, classical as well as folk dance. These were all things I had chosen not just because of my own interests but because of the nature of the company, the sense that it might just open up a certain kind of memory.

Current initiatives include a revival of the use of the London studio space for dramaturgical workshops of Asian script material. Does this mean new writing, or an exploration of the dramatic traditions of South Asia?

Both really, in that I think the new writing will be informed by an exploration of the traditions. I am convinced of the need once again to establish a core of performers who will be working on our aesthetics: it is not a question of 'doing Indian dramaturgy', but of discovering through that encounter what is ours. One of the thematic explorations I have in mind is something I am calling 'Journey to the West', which is really trying to construct what is the only epic of our times, the story of migration: of the arrival, and of the transformation that has occurred. And that offers possible references to a huge variety of texts, from the *Odyssey* to the *Ramayana*, which can help focus the explorations.

Is there any reason why Tara has not operated in the past as a forum for new writing?

The reason is tied up with the project: the obvious analogy would be, 'How can you contribute to others when you're not sure of yourself?' By now we are sure of the kind of territory we inhabit, the kinds of things that we want to do, the ways in which we want to do them. Therefore there's a clarity for new writers, and that's happening now. The first of the recent new plays is being done by an actor, Ravi Kapoor, who joined us in 1993 with *Heer Ranjha*, and remained associate with the company, and has written a text called *Oh Sweet Sita*, which he will have directed in April 1997.

This is his dialogue with the *Ramayana*, a cheeky look at the *Ramayana* – with a potentate of some northern city journeying down south to London and having these rites of passage. It's interesting that that kind of person has been influenced by the work of the company, and now has a context in which to place his work.

A second initiative addresses the problem of training Asian performers, in liaison with drama schools and with Equity. Can you identify difficulties (with intake or curriculum), and is there a policy you would like to see implemented?

What I consider to be the fundamental problem is to do with the curriculum. To a large extent drama schools are becoming functional, as education is generally. You have got three years, you do this kind of study, and then you become an accountant or some other functionary. I think that is against the spirit of education: education ought to be about the exercise of the imagination, about making oneself fit for whatever one decides to do in life. In the case of drama schools that's even more necessary. It is wrong that drama students – whether they're Asians or not – are denied their own heritage, and part of the heritage of modern theatre is its encounters with Asian theatre. They simply do not meet that in drama schools.

The encounters with Asian theatre date from the time of Artaud right through to Brook. The students come across all of those people, but don't acually go to the sources of these great practitioners. So one has a profession that is constantly reinforcing its narrowness of vision. That's my bone of contention with drama schools, and that's what I hope we can play a part in helping to change.

Has Tara had a high retention rate with performers and practitioners – or been subject over the years to the market in theatre and television?

I think on balance one could say that what has made the company is a good retention rate. Of course, we've lost people to television and to other theatres – mainly to television – but that's normal. I used to have lots of angst about it, but I don't any more, because I also accept the fact that we do manage to attract people who stay. And that has been a remarkable feat of the company. It's good from several points of view, but at the same time it poses challenges. The challenges come notably when the individual is not committed to a clear exploratory line in terms of dramaturgy, and then there are problems.

For myself, I've always had that sense that this is my home, these are the roots of my being, and that here are the creative tools that inspire me and that I feel comfortable with. Each of us in the theatre is looking for that kind of condition of relative comfort – not a comfort that is enervating, but a comfort which is a seedbed for ever better work.

You have written and spoken of Binglish as defining a certain kind of production as well as a certain kind of language. Can you explain?

Binglish communicates the sense that this is not English: it's a bastard English, or beastly English, a sense of wanting to be English. It comes really from a recognition of what's happened in England in the time that I've been here – now close on thirty years – which is that all purities or all notions of the authentic have been blown sky high. What is an authentic British diet, what is authentic English music, what is it to be the authentic Englishman? Who can with any truth, with any honesty, say what that is? All one can say is that there are fractures, there are fragments, there are Binglishes, really, in the very texture of our language.

Now that to some extent has occurred with the language throughout its history. It's accelerated because there is a physical expression of it now, because one can literally see the bodies from whose languages certain words have appeared in English. And those bodies are not content any longer simply to work in that received medium: those bodies are also wanting to bring their own languages into English, to some extent, and to make it a part of them. That needs a reflection in the theatre, but in terms of general theatre fare one sees little reflection of that reality. To me that seems deeply ironical, and deeply dishonest, particularly when the overriding convention is a realistic one. What realism are we presenting, when in fact the reality of life outside is not being reflected in our theatre productions?

Apart from Tagore, Salman Rushdie seems to be a major figure for you. I sense that this is the result of two different aspects – the first that of an Asian radical confronting history and tradition, the second that of a writer of Binglish?

Absolutely, and I'd add just one other thing, which is that Salman is *the* modern writer in the sense that the past and the present are leaking into each other in his work. The Asian who buys a house in the heart of Buckinghamshire, this leaking into a certain kind of quintessential notion of a southern Englishness. And Bangra music leaking into popular music, food leaking into the notion of what is an English diet. That sense of leaking is so critical in Salman. But I find an absolute empathy with him also because that is what is going on with us. Young actors are coming out of drama schools, and we find that it is either the Caribbean or India or Africa leaking into their present sensibility, which is Stanislavsky and Brecht, and whatever else they have done. That's where I think that what I long for and what I hope we will achieve is to become the theatrical equivalent of what Salman has so supremely articulated in literature.

Has the way Tara has been organized as a company changed over the years? Have there been political debates over the running of the company?

Not massive political debates, although I suppose there were more in the earlier times, as we were making the transition into a realization that aesthetics is a political position. Our aesthetics are informed by our politics and our politics are our aesthetics. In coming to that realization there were intense debates – such as who we should seek sponsorship from. Once Princess Di was to come to a centre we often rehearsed in, and there were debates as to whether we should do a presentation in front of her.

I think they were entirely valid discussions. But we did do a presentation, and of course we were nicely toyed with by Princess Di, who found it all terribly charming. What we'd presented was an extract from a production called *The Shape of Dreams*, which was about Asian women who were learning English. This was one of our first productions in which we also featured Indian languages, and the negotiation between Indian languages and English, and if I remember rightly she had this comment about, 'Do you all speak English so well?'

That sense of debate, while no longer so formal now, continues within the company, centred round the consequences of certain works: when looking back, after a work is finished, we ask: 'Should we be going down this road?' That is a continual discussion which has become part of the stuff of Tara, and goes on in between rehearsals, outside of rehearsals, in between other work. It's one of the things that contributes to our environment being so attractive to a certain type of individual.

Can we review here the problems you and Tara have experienced in the relations between theatrical activity and religious or communal feeling?

I think the essential problem is that we are inherently ambivalent, and our ambivalence is overt as well. The amibivalent relationship with the community has been there right from the beginning. We used to have discussions with the audience after every show, yet we reached a point three or four years into the beginning of our history where we stopped that practice, because we found it an impossible load.

It's not so easy to claim us for any section of any community. We are not overtly Indian in the sense of Hindus, we are not overtly Pakistani in the sense of Muslims, we are not overtly English in the sense of being white. But we are disturbingly a bit of everything, and that's what I mean by ambivalence. Yet we have also championed the notion of being Asian with integrity on the public stage. We've always done it on our own terms, without becoming part of any particular group.

At times there has been this sense of wanting to own us, of wanting to make a claim on us to be a part of something. Now that's a constant danger: in the same way as you must not be part of any one funder, but you do need to maintain a certain kind of relationship with funders, an allowance for a certain flow of funds. So with the community as well: we maintain contacts but fall a little short of delivering what they would ideally like us to deliver.

Sometimes it's exposed us to the heat. With the play *Sniffer Ganesha*, the intention was not to poke fun at Ganesha, but to use the imagery of the sensibility of the nose. For one local Hindu organization that was a travesty. Although basically they were seeking publicity for themselves, I had to recognize that there was this trend of feeling, and so I changed the title of the show to *Pinocchio Goes Asia*. But the show remained the same, and there was still a guy called Sniffer Ganesha. If the heat was dissipated by that, then fine.

Co-production has clearly been of major importance to Tara, as well as to many companies recently. How has this aspect developed, and how should it continue?

It's developed because of commercial necessity, since there isn't the finance now to do the kind of work you want to do without getting into bed with the bigger theatres. It has also been very useful, particularly the relationship with the National, and I hope mutually so. Strategically it has been very good for us: and for the National it has meant that there is an audience which is going to come in there which has not hitherto.

The danger is that, rather as with funding sources, you are in a dependency-culture: you know that this is an unequal relationship and you're fitting in to someone else's programme. Even though you're putting all your energies into that one piece of work, the theatre house can't do that, because you're just one of several others during the year. That's where I am increasingly coming to feel that the future survival of the company ultimately depends upon making institutional what has been the sensibility of the company, which is independence.

We have been constantly walking this tightrope, maintaining independent integrity, despite the vicissitudes of fashion and taste, and ploughing our own path. Now I think that that has got to be institution-alized, and that means we must have our own building. There is a delicious irony that I am talking of this on the fiftieth anniversary of the independence of India and Pakistan, and I think in some senses it's the same project. When you're independent, and you have your own house, then you're talking to another house on a condition of relative parity, rather than on the condition of being an itinerant beggar looking for the crumbs, looking for a little space.

Do you think Tara will have problems resisting a kind of commodification of its work by the theatrical and funding establishment?

Yes, the strength of Tara has lain in its ambivalence, its integrity. The integrity is based on the notion of the migrant, which is the consciousness of being fragments – which also mean that it's less easy to pigeon-hole us. At the moment the kind of pigeon-holing is that of being an Asian theatre company. Yet increasingly we ourselves, in our practices, are more and more prepared to shake even the funders' views of what is to be expected of Asian theatre.

One of the dangers of being in ambivalent territory is that you're not so commercially successful, because there's no defined market. And the next twenty years is going to be about making a success in commercial terms. For me, what that means is that I don't become reliant on any one big funder, which at the moment we are. So there would be lots of people who have stakes in us, but no one who had the biggest slice of the cake.

So you're saying that there's a kind of subsidized commodification as well as a market commodification, and that's a danger to be avoided?

Absolutely. But if one is clever it can be played with, and that fine tightrope is what we, like other theatre companies, are going to have to tread. It would be much easier in some senses for us to be a very defined, very clear, very obvious Indian theatre company: we would fit a niche, and I think we would survive very well. But with no real joy, and no real verve, and far too many headaches, because someone would own you.

Multicultural or intercultural – should we be using either term to describe the work of Tara, or should we be suspicious of both?

I think suspicious of both, and in some sense I've already begun to try to lay out a sort of answer to that. It is a journey that we are still making at Tara, to try and distinguish what kind of multiculturalism this is. One thing is certainly clear: we have gone very far away from the notion of multiculturalism as a social project. Multiculturalism only has cogency if it has an aesthetic articulation, an aesthetic basis. Otherwise it's simply a question of equal opportunities, and that's a different matter altogether. The aesthetics of multiculturalism is something else, and that should be the proper enquiry.

Magdalen Rubalcava
Resident Designer

Designing for Tara

I have worked with Tara Arts for over ten years, as the company's designer for most productions during that time. And one of the reasons that I enjoy working with Tara is that I can use my own mixed nationality both politically and artistically: I feel at home.

Almost invariably, the beginnings of any design for one of the company's productions are not based on a script, but on the story told by Jatinder, the director, to me. Neither Jatinder nor I see a 'set' in the conventional style of a 'West-End set', but as a piece of sculpture. It is important that, seen from any angle, both on-stage and off, the set has a visual beauty. As much of the set as possible must be available in rehearsal from day one, so that the actors' thoughts and feelings, as well as ideas from Jatinder and myself, are incorporated into the final version: and the design changes as rehearsals go on.

The process of producing a design for a Tara show can go through four or five different models: the final design is not only an amalgamation of those models, but may well include elements from past sets that we have not yet used. The sets invariably include elements that the audience may not or cannot see, but that have meaning for Jatinder, for myself, and for the actors. In *Le Bourgeois Gentilhomme*, for instance, there were perspex screens in the wings, painted to represent gardens drawn from Moghul prints. These were visible to the actors, but also gave the lighting designer the opportunity to use the colours of the screens like lighting gels, to spill colour on to the stage.

One of the perceptions about Tara's design is that the costume is 'Indian'. The reality, however, is that the source-images can also be Japanese, Chinese, and Eastern European. Any one costume may represent several characters – a coat may be turned inside-out or may be split in half. Underneath, the base-costume usually comprises Indian pyjamas, shirts or sari blouses, and a cummerband, on top of which is the main costume. This allows for fast changes of character, but also gives the costume a 'complete' look. As a consequence, all of Tara's costumes are made and not bought, and in their making it is important that an allowance is made for acrobatic movement and dance for all the shows.

Tara's costumes need to be elegant, colourful, and complete to reflect the way clothes are worn in India – as a statement as much as for their practicality. As a result, Tara has created its own fashion in costume: Tara's costumes are clothes, not just costumes.

Shelley King
Actor with Tara

Patel . . . and Not Patel

My relationship with Tara Arts began in 1989, with the production of *Danton's Death*. Jatinder had made it very clear that none of the assembled actors would know the roles they were to play until at least the third week of rehearsal. Unsure about this process, I scanned the list of Büchner's characters full of doubt. Then, in the certainty that none of them was called Patel, I decided to put whatever reputation I had amassed

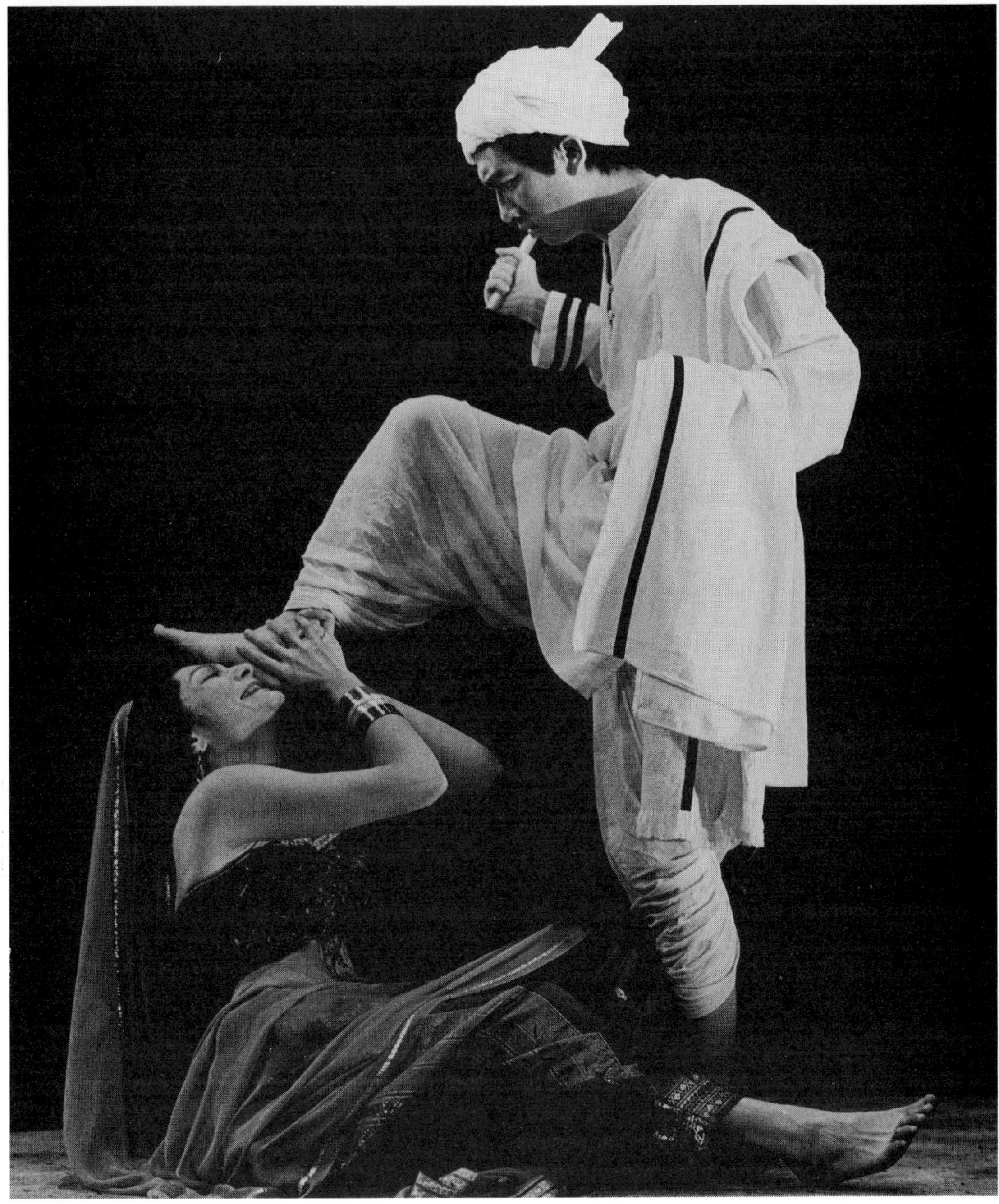

Shelley King (Heer) and David Tse (Ranjha) in *Heer Ranjha*, adapted and directed by Jatinder Verma (1991).

during my previous twelve years as an actor in Jatinder's hands. Patel is a fine name, but I had played four characters called Patel in the last twelve months, and was just about to play another. And I was feeling claustrophobic. In the end, Jatinder cast me as Robespierre opposite the splendid Muraly Menon from Trivandrum in South India, who played Danton. Since then I have played various characters of both genders for Jatinder and Tara, and I have visited countries and continents where I have worked with performers whose skill and knowledge have humbled me.

Since I began working with Tara, I have never had to play another Mrs. Patel.

Tara Arts: a Chronology of Funding

1979–80	Funding from Commission for Racial Equality for part-time administrative post.
1982–83	First project funding from Greater London Arts Association.
1983–84	GLC capital grant for purchase of the Earslfield building; revenue funding from Wandsworth Borough Council; project funding from GLAA.
1985–86	First revenue funding from Arts Council of Great Britain.
1987–88	First three-year franchise funding from ACGB.
1989–90	Wandsworth BC cuts its grant.
1990–91	Three-year franchise funding from ACGB.
1993–94	Revenue funding from Arts Council of England for one year; first commercial sponsorship (from Manchester Airports).
1994–95	Three-year franchise funding from ACE; sponsorship from Michelob.
1997–98	Three-year franchise funding from ACE, including 30 per cent increase to 'build on national touring work, and to support the company's development under the lottery stabilization project'.

Matthew Jones
Administrator

Funding a 'Company of Identity'

In one sense Tara belongs to a loose grouping which could be described as 'companies of identity', which might include the Black Theatre Co-operative, Sphinx (formerly the Women's Theatre Group), Graeae, and Gay Sweatshop. The classic funding pattern here is that the company is initially founded by individuals with shared educational, cultural and political backgrounds: then, after a number of projects or productions, the group receives funding for a specific proposal, either from a special-interest organization, a trust, or local government.

The next grant will be for a larger project, and may include a greater contribution to administrative costs. At this stage the company may seek to professionalize its members, and establish a legal status. Companies may remain at this level for some time: but larger project funds may be followed by an accumulation of disparate funders, and the possibility of sponsorship.

The key developmental moment is applying for and receiving revenue funding, which demonstrates the funder's willingness to recognize the identity of the organization, rather than the value of any individual project. The final stage within the current system is what is called the 'franchise', where the Arts Council of England will offer support for periods of three years at a time.

In Tara's case, the initial funding was from the Committee for Racial Equality, and early grants to Tara were a reflection of the company's community base – its commitment to centres of Asian population, primarily in London. In particular, the Labour Greater London Council in the 1980s was proactive in its policy of promoting Asian organizations, and there was a substantial expansion of funded black and Asian companies during that period.

With the loss of its local funding from Wandsworth in 1990-91, Tara's national touring work became its sole area of operation. The justification for the cut was, ironically, that Tara was now of national significance, and inappropriate for local funding! As a result, the Earlsfield building was closed, and the TIE and community groups were disbanded. Only recently, through its success in earning income and gaining charitable support, has the company been able to rebuild community work and a substantial commitment to theatre for children.

Vincent Ebrahim
Actor and Artistic Associate

Messing with Molière

I came from Cape Town, South Africa, to Britain in 1976, after graduating at a drama school, and for the next fifteen years worked for InterAction, Common Stock, Joint Stock, the RSC, and the National, and in other theatres. In 1990 I began my association with Tara Arts by playing the Mayor in Gogol's *The Government Inspector*.

When I joined Tara Arts I felt I had 'come home' as a performer. Even though I am a South African, I found that I had much in common with a group of mainly Indian actors, not least our experience of Britain. I was working with a group of people with whom I did not feel the need continually to justify my presence: my 'history' was taken for granted, my 'strangeness' was no longer estrangement. As an actor I was returning 'into my skin', where before I had played characters so many times removed from myself and from my experience of the world.

Working with Tara, the artistic challenges that were set were explored in an atmosphere of mutuality. Tara was setting out the criteria by which it was to be judged by searching for the appropriate theatrical language to express what it wanted to say. And if that language did not exist, it would be necessary to invent it!

Interpreting European classics such as *Tartuffe*, *The Government Inspector*, *Oedipus the King*, and *Le Bourgeois Gentilhomme* as Tara has done over recent years is the act of 'inhabiting the language' and, by extension, the culture of Europe: laying claim to it, appropriating it, and subtly pushing at the envelope of the cultural consciousness of Britain from the inside. In Tara's version of *Le Bourgeois Gentilhomme*, the action was transposed to seventeenth-century Pondicherry, then a French colony in south India. The target for the satire was a wealthy fisherman, Kaka Deen, who was aiming to reinvent himself in the colonizers' image.

Coming from South Africa, all this rang a few bells. My own family had been subject to these pressures. My mother and her sister had different racial classifications, determined by the marriages they had contracted into – my mother 'of mixed race', my aunt 'white' because she had married an Italian before the race classification laws reached the statute books. They lived in adjacent neighbourhoods, segregated by the Group Areas Act which forbade them living in the same street!

In playing Kaka Deen, I invested the character with attributes that drew on these observations: his pedantic and dogmatic manner, his irritation with his wife's wish to remain closely tied to the community they came from, his prejudice against and aversion to anything 'black'.

For Further Reading

Compiled by Sophie Robson

BACKGROUND

The Arts and Ethnic Minorities Plan (Arts Council of Great Britain, 1986).
Arts Without Frontiers (Arts Council of Great Britain, 1990).
Naseem Khan, *The Arts Britain Ignores: the Art of Ethnic Minorities* (Arts Council of Great Britain, 1976).
Kwesi Owusu, ed., *The Struggle for Black Arts in Britain* (Comedia, 1986).
Kwesi Owusu, ed., *Storms of the Heart: an Anthology of Black Arts and Culture* (Camden Press, 1988).
Towards Cultural Diversity (Arts Council of Great Britain, 1989).

JATINDER VERMA AND TARA ARTS

Marianne Brace, 'After Bollywood, Binglish', *The Independent*, 9 November 1994.
Maria Delgado and Paul Heritage, eds., 'Jatinder Verma', in *In Contact with the Gods? Directors Talk Theatre* (Manchester University Press, 1996).
Sophie Robson, *Tara Arts: a Victim of Its Own Success?* (MA Thesis, City University, 1991).
Edmond Rostand, *Cyrano*, adapted by Jatinder Verma and Ranjit Bolt (Absolute Classics, 1995).
Jatinder Verma, 'Transformations in Culture: the Asian in Britain', *Proceedings of the Royal Society of Arts* (1989).
Jatinder Verma, 'Crossing the Border: an Encounter with Odysseus', address given at Portland State University, July 1994.
Jatinder Verma, 'Asian Theatre in Britain: Historical Developments and Contemporary Identity', address given at the University of Birmingham, October 1994.
Jatinder Verma, 'Binglish: a Jungli Approach to Multicultural Theatre', *Studies in Theatre Production*, No. 13 (1996).
Jatinder Verma, 'The Challenge of Binglish: Analyzing Multicultural Productions', in Patrick Campbell, ed., *Analyzing Performance* (Manchester University Press, 1996).
Jatinder Verma, 'Punjabi Theatre in Britain: Context and Challenge', address to the Punjabi Theatre Conference, London, September 1996.
James Woodall, 'An Indian Gentilhomme', *The Observer*, 30 October 1994.

Tara Arts Website: http://www.tara-arts.com

Photo credits for this feature: Carol Baugh (page 361), John Haynes (page 363), and Hugo Glendinning (pages 363 and 369).

Catherine Diamond

The Pandora's Box of 'Doi Moi': the Open-Door Policy and Contemporary Theatre in Vietnam

In the 1990s, Vietnamese traditional theatre has seen its popular base eroded by foreign videos, television imports, and the films that have poured into the country since the advent of the 'open door' policy, or *doi moi*. As that policy is primarily economic in purpose, the advantages offered to the national culture have been questionable. The traditional forms here discussed by Catherine Diamond – *tuong*, *hat boi*, and *cheo* – have lost much of their status in the urban areas, though still popular in the countryside. However, the forms which address contemporary issues – 'renovated theatre' (*cai luong*), spoken theatre (*kich noi*), and, most recently, 'mini-theatre' (*san khau nho*) – play to significant numbers in Saigon and Hanoi, often employing a distinctive vein of satirical humour. Though trained in the academies of the Soviet Union and Eastern Europe, Vietnamese dramatists have now broken away from the socialist realist ideal and are looking towards the West and China for new artistic developments. The author of this survey, Catherine Diamond, is a dancer and drama professor in Taiwan. She has recently published *Sringara Tales*, a collection of short stories about the traditional dancers in Southeast Asia.

ALTHOUGH the 'open-door' policy, or *doi moi*, was largely adopted by the Vietnamese because other socialist and former socialist countries were encouraging free market economies, and Vietnam's own economy needed a radical opening-up to stimulate it, party leaders were not unaware of the risk posed by the policy to the traditional and developing national culture. A draft report of the Eighth Party Congress made in June 1996 stated that culture was of particular importance during the *doi moi* period:

> Culture is the spiritual foundation of society, a moving force to promote the socio-economic development and a target of socialism. All short- and long-termed cultural activities should be aimed toward a modern culture combined with a strong national character. They should inherit and bring into play moral and aesthetic values as well as the cultural and artistic legacy of the nation.   Le Minh Ly, 1996

During both the French and American Wars, culture was closely connected to revolutionary tasks. Ho Chi Minh said, 'Culture should be a front in which writers and artists are soldiers.' But the revolution is over, and the government wants to encourage economic growth on all fronts while maintaining control of outside cultural influence. On one hand, given the potential menace of foreign cultural dominance, the government's anxiety is not unfounded; on the other, it has given mixed signals to artists within the country – or, as one director put it, '*doi moi* is the opening of one door and closing of another'.[1]

Most dramatists concede, however, that during the past four or five years they have been able to explore a wider range of topics which before were considered not so much taboo as merely irrelevant, but they are still subject to arbitrary and shifting guidelines as the door sits ajar. Policy makers do not have a long-term plan for cultural development but tend to act and react. The uncertainty in regard to increased openness can be seen in the occasional launching of anti-cultural pollution campaigns – or in the attitude toward satellite dishes, which last year were appearing on propaganda posters as part of the vision of the future, but are now being removed – since the government realized it would not be desirable for the masses to have unlimited access to unregulated information.[2]

Since the early 1990s, Vietnam has been inundated with videos from Hong Kong, Taiwan, Singapore, and the USA, as well as its own locally made low-budget videos. This has affected the entire entertainment industry. Not only the theatre, but Vietnamese film and television have suffered. Audiences find the local offerings boring and of poor quality. Large amounts of money have been poured into political blockbusters, such as *A Nation Rises Up*, which fail to recoup even a fraction of their cost. Critics are blunt about the films coming out of the state companies, asking, 'How soon can our films become less insipid?' (Thanh, 1996).

The implementation of a new television channel, VTV3, attempted to get away from the old-fashioned hackneyed dramas by offering 'a wide range of programmes dealing with students, businessmen, teachers, small vendors, cyclo drivers, shopkeepers, whom the new relations generated by the market economy have pushed into untenable, even tragic, situations which are often left unresolved by the scriptwriters. But these too, have now lost the public's interest' (Huy, 1996).

Fate of the Traditional Forms

Set in this context, the theatre reflects both the struggles and the triumphs of a once-popular performance art. Traditional Vietnamese styles of musical theatre – namely *tuong* (the classical theatre originally influenced by thirteenth-century Chinese texts and performance styles, but also mixed with Indian and Cham gesturing and music) and *cheo*, the northern indigenous folk theatre – are losing ground.

Tuong, called *hat boi* in the South, is suffering from a lack both of students and audiences.[3] Once the popular opera of the courts, its plots of grotesque demonstrations of loyalty to authority seem out of keeping with a society surging toward modernity. Contemporary writers do not write scripts for *tuong*, which thus remains in a preser-

Above: an outdoor performance in Hanoi by Nha Hat Tuong Trung Uong in the traditional, Chinese-influenced *tuong* style – once widely popular, but now facing a decline in audiences.

Below: Ho Chi Minh City's *hat boi* troupe, Doan Nghe Thuat Hat Boi Thanh Pho Ho Chi Minh, performs the patriotic play, *Bong Hong nui Nua*, about a Vietnamese heroine, Trieu Thi Trinh, who triumphs over a Chinese villain (with moustache).

vationist mode. While masters of *tuong* still perform, there are fewer and fewer young performers and the general level of artistry is in decline.

Cheo, on the other hand, which once thrived in the villages around Hanoi, has become uprooted. Once the provenance of the villagers, who themselves performed at festivals such as those held after Tet, it is now performed more and more by hired professional city troupes, whose employment reflects favourably on the village's economic status. Since it has no known external influences, *cheo* has been embraced as the national theatre, and *cheo* troupes, like those of water puppetry, are sent abroad to represent Vietnam at international workshops and festivals.

Unlike *tuong*, which supports the moral status quo, *cheo* has always been a satiric form, featuring strong female characters, a clown-figure, called the *he* or *lao*, and off-stage voices which interact with on-stage characters.[4] The humour of *cheo* has allowed it the flexibility and also the adaptability to comment on modern situations. It was originally a scriptless, improvised form, although a few *cheo* texts have become classics. Very few writers now write for *cheo*, however; the scripts are difficult because they include portions of verse, and modern *cheo* has never been as popular as the more traditional renditions.[5]

There has been some attempt to wed *cheo* performance style with western texts, and dramatists still refer to a experiment of the 1980s in which East Germans and Vietnamese collaborated on a *cheo* version of Brecht's *Caucasian Chalk Circle*. In January 1997 another collaboration took place when Ellen Stewart of New York's La Mama integrated techniques of *cheo* and Vietnam's water puppets to produce a new work entitled *Dionysus*. Her performance, however, does not seem to have had much of an impact on the Hanoi theatre scene, and Vietnamese dramatists have reacted indifferently to it. It was an isolated experiment, which, like so many multicultural programmes, used traditional Asian forms to clothe a western product.

Dramatists in the three modern genres, *cai luong* (renovated opera), *kich noi* (realistic spoken drama), and *san khau nho* (mini-theatre) have fared better in both developing their texts and performing their craft, but they must still steer a course between government restrictions and a public that wants entertainment, usually comic, above everything else. What some dramatists have a particularly difficult time in dealing with is the current 'appearance of openness'.

The 'Appearance of Openness'

Satirical performances on official corruption and increasingly materialist values are popular, especially in Saigon, and social and political issues are played with surprising alacrity on stages in the South. For example, during the same week in February 1997 that a trial of a major corruption scandal was handing down death sentences to the main perpetrators, satirical reviews in Ho Chi Minh City's large municipal theatre were amusing sell-out audiences with the vagaries of the justice system and endemic official corruption. While this seemed to come close to attacking the government – rather than merely the vice of corruption – such a perspective was qualified by the comments of the Saigon director and playwright, Nguyen Thi Minh Ngoc. In 1975, she said, the US government had given money to students to stage anti-government plays to create the appearance of openness.

In the 1980s, she herself belonged to a troupe that performed political and social satires, but quit when she realized that it was being manipulated by the government. She is deeply suspicious of these appearances of openness and the deception they perpetuate, making real freedom of expression all the more difficult to attain. When she voiced a desire to produce *Waiting for Godot*, she was told by a cultural official, 'Over my dead body.' Beckett and Ionesco have been singled out for particular odium by the government, which reasons that the former socialist countries of Eastern Europe allowed performances of their works, and look what has happened to them![6]

Still, despite these obvious limitations of a cautious and often arbitrarily vigilant government, and the demands of an audience desiring temporary distraction, some performances have captured the popular imagination and achieved an admirable degree of artistic merit.[7] Among the most vital modern theatres in the country are the Youth Theatre (Nha Hat Tuoi Tre) in Hanoi that premieres new *kich noi*; the 'mini-theatre', the Nghiem Theatre Club (Cau Lac Bo San Khau The Nghiem) in Ho Chi Minh City, that provides a permanent home for contemporary experimental productions; and Tran Huu Trang Cai Luong Theatre (Nha Hat Cai Luong Tran Huu Trang), one of the longest running and most successful *cai luong* troupes.[8] These theatres have the best stock of talented actors and directors, attract the best new playwrights, and have built up steady and loyal audiences.[9]

Kich noi, the spoken drama, emerged during the early part of this century. It is considered a wholly new genre in Vietnam because it was a foreign implant, initially imitating the theatre of the colonial powers, and then, ironically, conscripted to serve in the fight against colonialism. Its development began from the translation and adaptation of French classical theatre, popular French melodramas, and the new socio-political realistic dramas of the Ibsen school. Appearing in 1907, Molière's *The Miser* was among the first plays to be staged in Vietnamese (Mackerras, p. 8). Then, during the 'thirties and 'forties, when the French colonial government increasingly repressed democratic movements in Vietnam while fighting the fascist powers in Europe, *kich noi* was appropriated by Vietnamese intellectuals to express new ideas about both modern society and nationhood.

In the 'fifties and 'sixties, Russian plays began to be translated, and socialist realist models were imitated *en masse*, but now they are less popular than Russian classics. In 1996, Tran Minh Ngoc, one of the foremost directors in Ho Chi Minh City, was preparing *Uncle Vanya*, along with *The Tempest* and *A Streetcar Named Desire*. Many European and American realistic plays have

Director Pham Thi Thanh addressing the audience at the beginning of *Vu Nhu To.*

been translated, but few plays after the 1960s are known, and virtually no modern Vietnamese plays have been translated into western languages.[10]

A Nationalistic Classic

Pham Thi Thanh, wh is the most celebrated woman director in Hanoi, and currently chairwoman of the Youth Theatre, recently tested the waters of *doi moi's* political liberality by premiering one of Vietnam's most famous early spoken dramas. The historical writer Nguyen Huy Tuong (1912-60) wrote two celebrated *kich noi*: *Vu Nhu To* (the name of the protagonist), and *Bac Son* (North Mountain, the home of a guerrilla group against the French). Although *Bac Son* premiered in Hanoi in 1945 to considerable acclaim, *Vu Nhu To*, written in 1942, was not performed until 1995. After Pham obtained permission to begin work on the play, she remained apprehensive about how it would be received by the government and public, while her actors were troubled by the conflicting and contradictory ideological messages of the play.

While ostensibly pro-nationalistic, *Vu Nhu To* shows a pre-socialist perspective. Influenced by bourgeois realism, it celebrates individual vision and the necessary stubbornness to pursue that vision. Based on an historical incident, the play is about a peasant, Vu Nhu To, who showed a genius for building, and was was employed by the Emperor Le Tuong Duc (1510-16), the decadent last king of the illustrious Le dynasty, to build a magnificent palace.

Because the king is a corrupt and vicious tyrant, Vu Nhu To refuses, but is finally persuaded to go ahead with the plan, not by the king's threats – which include the killing of his mother – but by the blandishments of his first wife, Dan Thiem, who inspires him by saying that he should build the palace for the country rather than the king. The king will soon die, but the palace, standing for generations, will remain the pride of the Vietnamese people.

Vu is initially liked by his peasant workmen, but as he is increasingly seen as a vehicle for the king's tyranny, they turn against him. Both Vu and Dan Thiem are killed when a general, taking advantage of the people's discontent, rebels against the king, and the half-finished palace collapses in flames.

The play illustrates the problematic position of the creative artist in an authoritarian state, where he is caught between a corrupt king, ignorant masses, ambitious military, and needy family. Moreover, any symbol of power on stage can be read as the current government, which Pham was concerned would bristle at such an implicit critique, especially if made by a representative of contemporary intellectuals, restless following decades of restraint.

At one point, Vu stands alone on stage, contemplating Dan Thiem's proposal, and then sinks down onto the king's empty throne. This brought gasps from the audience, which quite clearly read the move as a challenge to the ruling power. Vu's position is also difficult and suspect. It reveals that all the professions are mere servants of power, without autonomous integrity. Their dependence on the whims of the rich as well as on the fickle loyalties of the peasants undermines their ability to effect change and alter the status quo.

But Tham's production had a still more probing critique. The performance begins with a film of a naked man hacking at an enormous expanse of barren sunbaked soil. The film juxtaposes his effort with its futility. This, according to Pham, reflects most people's lives: they remain on the level of mere survival, their vision unable to extend beyond that of obtaining the next meal. In contrast, Vu Nhu To and Dan Thiem are the persecuted visionaries who look into the future and try to see the larger picture of humankind.

The film then shows selected glimpses of important monuments around the world – the Pyramids, the Great Wall, the Taj Mahal, the Forbidden City, Angkor Wat, alongside pictures of great artists such as Mozart and Van Gogh. What is conspicuously absent is any contribution from Vietnam. Where are its monuments? Who are its internationally recognized geniuses? More specifically, why has its feudalism, unlike that of China, its giant neighbour to the north, not produced great works? Has it been lacking in vision, or, as in the case of Vu Nhu To, has it killed off its visionaries?

The Emergence of 'Mini-Theatre'

This is the profoundly disturbing question the production asks its audience. The role of the intellectual/artist is one that remains as much a problem in the socialist state as in the former feudal one. Moreover, the film bespeaks the continued ambivalence of Vietnam towards China, with whom it shares so much, historically and culturally. But as Vietnam emerges from its own civil strife it is attempting to carve out a distinct niche, in which its indigenous arts such as *cheo* and *roi nuoc* (water puppetry) have assumed a new importance. Although the government is nervous about the current impact of the West, the more deep-seated confrontation is, and perhaps will always be, with China, both because of its ominous proximity and its overwhelming immensity.

Top: Thi Nhien (Minh Hang), the favourite concubine of the King, Le Tuong Duc (Chi Trung), entertains him with a dance in *Vu Nhu To*. Bottom: the King visits Vu Nhu To (Anh Tu) while the construction of his magnificent palace is still proceeding well.

During the past five years, a new kind of theatre has become popular in the two largest cities – the 'mini' or 'experimental' theatre. Although initially rejected by audiences who found it too strange, *san khau nho* performances are now sold-out affairs. The term 'mini-theatre' implies a genre that is both contingent on its space – small and informal – and experimental in style.

'Mini-theatre' also means making do with little – minimal set and props, no backdrop, no stage furniture, no microphones. With the plays generally being set in contemporary times, the actors often wear their own clothes as costumes, while the 'stage' is assembled out of two or three platforms covered with cloth. The 240 spectators in the theatre of the Nghiem Theatre Club surround the performing space on three, sometimes four sides, and sit very close, thereby occupying the same space.[11]

While this theatre is considered avant garde in Vietnam, it does not embrace a policy of bizarre, threatening, or alienating expression at the expense of its audience's understanding and enjoyment.[12] It is still essentially popular theatre, full of tears and laughter, touching upon issues of immediate interest, but presenting its material with natural and subtle acting, and a great degree of verbal wit.

Director Tran Minh Ngoc recognizes that people still come to the theatre for entertainment, and that such a requirement is not incompatible with serious thought. One of the purposes of theatre, he says, is to distract the audience, to allow it some intellectual space away from the practical demands of daily life to contemplate the ethical and the aesthetic.

Hearing the Drums at Night, Thinking of Past Love (*Da co hoai lang*), written by Thanh Hoang, has been a very popular experimental piece since it premiered in 1994. The title is a line from the most beloved *cai luong* song of all time, 'Vong co' ('Reminiscences'). The story is about a Viet Kieu family – Vietnamese who have immigrated to the United States – and opens with the young American-born daughter preparing a surprise birthday for her boy-friend, who has recently made her first trip back to visit Vietnam. She has baked a birthday cake, speaks in English, and welcomes him with a sexual warmth that would be considered indecorous for a girl raised in Vietnam. Her boyfriend, wearing an I LOVE SAIGON tee-shirt, is overflowing with impressions he wants to share with her, but she is not interested.

In the household, we see neither father nor mother, but the grandfather, Mr. Tu, who has been a famous *cai luong* actor in Saigon. He is visited by a childhood friend, Mr. Nam. Both elderly men were only recently brought to the States by their sons, who themselves had made the voyage by boat much earlier. Tu and Nam offer comfort to one another, knowing they can never truly adapt to their new foreign home.

The girl and her grandfather display some good-natured antagonism, but the generation gap is exacerbated by their identity formation in two distinct cultures. The grandfather and his friend reminisce until Tu decides to use the cake and candles for a ceremony to the spirit of his dead wife.

Then a crisis occurs when the grand-daughter discovers that her birthday cake has been used for this ghost ceremony and rails at her grandfather. As he leaves, Tu hands her a notebook, her father's diary of his escape from Vietnam, telling of his companions in the boat being killed by pirates so that he remained the lone survivor. She is dazed by the revelation of what he endured, and the scene ends with the song 'Sometimes I Feel Like a Motherless Child'.

The next scene cuts to a winterscape and the two old men romp on a roof-top in their first experience of snow – the platforms simply being covered with a white cloth. Tu, inspired by the new sensation, enters into his former *cai luong* roles, dramatically gesturing and reciting, while Nam haplessly attempts to imitate him. They dance, slip, and slide like two ten-year-olds, seemingly happy for the first time. The grand-daughter comes out to apologize, but during her speech, Tu – who has had a tubercular cough throughout – slumps, his back to the audience, and dies.

Although virtually all the play's dialogue is comic, throughout Tu sings snatches of the 'Vong co', a song – expressing greater sorrow than simple sadness – which has brought audiences to tears since it was written in 1920 by Cao Van Lau, and which appears in almost every *cai luong*.[13] Here, the song is the epitome of nostalgic feeling, not only for the character stranded in America, but for the audience that remained behind. Without an ocean to separate them from the constant struggle of daily life in Vietnam, those watching the performance vicariously experienced through Tu's nostalgia their own mixed emotions about their severed past.

Unlike the rather stiff and stylized acting of the spoken drama, the acting in mini-theatre is more natural, and the best actors are very finely developed character actors.[14] The audience was totally engrossed in this performance; no one yawned or looked away, most of the time people were laughing at the banter between Nam and Tu, but it was obvious that these two characters were very close to people's hearts. The younger generation was not blamed for having interests elsewhere; the play was not about who was at fault, or the loss of traditional values or virtues; it was a tale of change, and how difficult it is for all people to adapt to the changes occurring around them. It was not lost on the audience that the representative of the best of the old Vietnam was a *cai luong* actor.

The Absence of Bitterness

The play, although still popular with audiences in 1997, was criticized by a few of the Viet Kieu who saw it. They said the older people now living in the United States do not regret leaving their homeland, since when they left it was in such a terrible state. They suggest that the nostalgia depicted in the play is to comfort those who remained behind, rather than accurately to represent the attitudes of those who feel lucky enough to have left.

Although one can sense an underlying current of resentment tinged with jealousy

Two scenes from *Da Co Hoai Lang*. Top: Tu (Thanh Loc) and Nam (Viet Anh) conduct a prayer ceremony to Tu's deceased wife. Bottom: The granddaughter (Hong Van) is upset at the desecration of her birthday cake by her grandfather (Thanh Loc) and Nam.

against the Viet Kieu, assigning blame for social ills is not the focus of contemporary Vietnamese theatre. Several outside commentators have noted, with some surprise, that although twentieth-century Vietnamese theatre has reflected the vicissitudes of the country, it currently shows little bitterness towards the outside aggressors of the past. As Colin Mackerras put it in 1987:

Considering the passions and bloodshed which politics have occasioned in Vietnam in this century, what strikes me most strongly is the lightness of the propaganda content and the absence of class or foreign enemies. Even in anti-Chinese dramas, the enemy does not appear much, and there do not appear to be many French or American villains in contemporary Vietnamese plays.   (Mackerras, p. 23)

There is more sadness than acrimony in the plays that contemplate the past. In the current productions, everyone is flawed, but no nationality or group is consistently singled out for blame. Judgement is not called for, but an understanding of these characters caught in dilemmas which are both individualized and emblematic of larger conflicts.

Neither writers nor theatre companies express any inclination to indulge in the post-colonial malaise of revelling in their victimization by foreign powers.[15] Instead, plays are critical of internal anti-social trends – such as rampant materialism in *The Misunderstood Devotion* (*Bau tren co dan*, 1996), Ai Nhu's drama about the demise of a *cai luong* theatre company in the new get-rich-quick society, or Hong Ngat's drama *Flying to Paradise* (*Len Tien*, 1994) about the frightening increase of heroin addiction plaguing Vietnam's urban youth.

Some of the older dramatists, members of the Association for Art and Literature,[16] who fought on the cultural front in the American War, see the theatre in a new phase. During the war, propaganda plays focused on the efforts of the soldier and guerrilla fighter. After the war, plays rather emphasized the plight of women – the widowed, homeless, childless, poor, and ill. Now many *cai luong*, *kich noi*, and mini-theatre productions centre on family reunions and reconciliations. Long lost spouses and children are found through convoluted plots fraught with coincidence and traumatic recognitions; or warring family factions are reconciled through the birth of a new child, signalling a determined optimism and hope for the future.[17]

The House with No Men (*Ngoi nha khong co dan ong*, 1993), as staged by the Nghiem Theatre Club, has been one of the most popular mini-theatre plays on this theme. Running continuously in Saigon for four years, not only has the original mini-theatre form created by Ngoc Linh been successful, but the *cai luong* version performed by the Tran Huu Trang Cai Luong Theatre has become a favourite, demonstrating how *cai luong* parallels and adapts other texts. The two versions use the same script, the mini-theatre version stressing the comic and the *cai luong* focusing on the melodramatic.

In Ho Chi Minh City, *cai luong*, a musical theatre that emerged during the First World War, has continued to be the most popular theatre despite the socialist government's disapproval of its lachrymose tendencies. *Cai luong* troupes perform throughout the country, but predominate in the South, and Ho Chi Minh City remains the centre for *cai luong* video production.

The Dual Nature of 'Cai Luong'

Some theories suggest that the origin of *cai luong* lay in the fusion of French popular music with the amateur chamber music of south and central Vietnam. By 1915-16, performers were linking songs with mimetic gestures as preludes and entire acts to circuses and motion picture shows. A year or two later, *cai luong* troupes appeared with the first plays based on well-known verse stories.[18] In the 1930s, *Cai luong* also incorporated music from the Cantonese theatre which performed in Cholon, the Chinese district of Saigon. The historical *cai luong* plays also borrowed the stylized costumes, gestures, and painted scenery from the Cantonese opera (Mackerras, p. 7).

One peculiar aspect of *cai luong* is that it embraces two distinctly different types of plots and presentation styles – one played in contemporary dress with its plots focusing on contemporary social and domestic problems, the other based on historical episodes, adapted from *hat boi*. One socialist critic ascribes the dual nature of *cai luong* to the influence of French colonialism, saying that it originated in improvised gestures about actual topics of the day to accompany the music. When it began edging toward a more consolidated form of national theatre, the French censors curtailed its populist leanings by insisting it depict themes in 'Chinese feudal history and Roman antiquity, while indulging in languorous lamentations with a view to encouraging the apathy of an urban audience more or less won over to a bourgeois way of life' (The Gioi, p. 225). This would explain the strange phenomenon of the *tuong lama* (transliteration of 'Roma'), the sub-genre of *cai luong* set in ancient Rome.[19]

After Vietnam's victory over France in 1954, there was an attempt to revamp *cai luong*, especially its 'mawkish, maudlin, and negative character', since it was no longer appropriate expression of a liberated people involved in the positive activity of nation building. The critic Tu Luong contends that the opera was successfully 're-renovated' in the North under Ho Chi Minh's control, becoming 'pure, wholesome, edifying, and attractive,' while it was becoming artistically stagnant in the South under the US puppet regime (p. 59). Foreign observers have also commented on its commerciality and poor quality during this period (Bowers, p. 37; Brandon, 1967, p. 74).

After the end of the American War in 1975, the contact between the northern and southern *cai luong* performers resulted in a renewed invigoration. In 1992, out of a total of 156 government supported groups, 86 are *cai luong*, 32 are *kich noi*, nineteen are *cheo*, nine are *tuong* and the remaining ten include puppetry, circus, and folk art groups. These figures do not include the many privately run commercial *cai luong* troupes (Janaczewska, p. 161).

Currently, *cai luong* thrives on the texts of other genres and media, and is constantly adapting the stories and plots of popular

From *The House with No Men*. Top: the fat woman (Mai Thanti Dung) carries her young fiancé (Minh Nhi) to Mrs. Hau's tailor's shop. Bottom: Summer (Ai Nhu) flirts with Fall's boyfriend (Minh Hoang).

novels, films, and plays, both foreign and local. Since its inception, *cai luong* has been eclectic and parasitical, absorbing any and all texts into its musical format, always emphasizing the sad and the sentimental.[20]

The House with No Men is a Vietnamese *House of Bernarda Alba*. It involves an overbearing mother, Mrs. Hau, and her three unmarried daughters – Spring, Summer, and Fall – and her unmarried younger sister, Di Ba. Mrs. Hau, a tailor, despises men because her husband attempted to flee Vietnam with another woman, both having been drowned at sea. Her antipathy affects the behaviour of her girls in different ways. The eldest, Spring, has a boy-friend but, influenced by her mother, she puts him off. The middle sister, Summer, is a witty nymphomaniac who enjoys taunting all men, currently toying with an elderly wealthy beau. Fall, the youngest, is the most seriously attached to her young man, but when she finds herself pregnant tries to commit suicide. Her boy-friend saves her, but she is cast out by her mother, and goes off, condemned to live in poverty with him.

The sisters struggle against their mother and their own anxieties. Mrs. Hau is implacable, however, and refuses to accept her youngest daughter's condition, even when she has a bad dream and is visited by her husband's ghost, which accuses her of tormenting her daughters with her own misguided and anti-life prejudices. The conflict is resolved when a son is born to Fall and Mrs. Hau is torn between her desire for a grandson and being unable to accept her son-in-law; finally the family is reunited by the new generation.

The mini-theatre version, aside from being a humorous social critique, was also viewed as a political allegory; the impotent men, such as Summer's boy-friend leaving for Paris or the father dying at sea with his lover or Fall's young husband languishing in poverty, are thus perceived as a commentary on the hamstrung country and as an implicit criticism of those who left and are still leaving.

Similarly, on one level the mother's hatred of men suggests the government's repressive actions that curtailed the aspirations of the younger generation – the daughter's. On a more personal level, the play expresses antagonism towards those whose bitterness from the past not only cripples themselves but destroys the lives of those around them. The mother's acceptance of the grandchild strikes a note of optimism for the future of *doi moi*, the prevailing 'open-door policy' in Vietnam.

The Versions Compared

The *cai luong* version of *The House with No Men* opened almost simultaneously with the mini-theatre version, and has proved equally popular. In 1996, it was being reset by the Tran Huu Trang Cai Luong Theatre, while the mini-theatre play was showing weekly. And while Nguyen Thi Minh Ngoc directed and performed in the mini-theatre version, she was also playing the same character of the unmarried sister in the *cai luong* directed by Hoa Ha. This is not the first time the two women directors have collaborated: in 1993 they worked in tandem on two versions of Cao Yu's play *Thunderstorm* (*Leiyu*, 1935), perhaps the most famous spoken drama in the Chinese repertoire.[21]

In the *cai luong*, the humour of *san khau nho* is held much in abeyance as it emphasizes the tearful melodrama of the mother's desertion by her husband and the daughters' pitiful struggles. Most of the scenes are weepy and histrionic. For example, when Summer finds herself rejected by her suitor, she flings a chair across the room and breaks down in a tantrum of self-pity. When Fall attempts to drink poison, her boy-friend stops her and sobbingly convinces her to have the baby. And the final reconciliation happens only after much tearful pleading without any comic relief. The tunes of the orchestra wind in and out of the action so that there is no break between an actor singing and speaking. And not only does the singing emerge quite naturally, but the instrumental music sustains the mood throughout the scene.

The two versions make an interesting study of contrasts around the same plot line.

The spider's web encloses Tu Le as Mrs. Hau (centre), Kim Xuan as Spring, and Nguyen Thi Minh Ngoc (with glasses), also the director of the play, as Di Ba, in *The House with No Men.*

The humour and naturalistic acting of mini-theatre demonstrate artistic restraint, while *cai luong*, on the contrary, casts restraint to the winds, with the actors revelling in their exhibitions of unabashed emotion. Both are popular, however, and *cai luong* continues to survive, if not thrive, because it is always able to incorporate into its action the favourite topic of the day.

Despite these recent developments, Vietnamese dramatists feel they have been very cut off from theatrical progress in other countries, except for Russian social-realist drama which no longer has any credibility for Vietnamese audiences. When its former allies in the Warsaw Pact countries became democratic, Vietnam was cut adrift economically and culturally, and now Vietnamese dramatists are turning to former colonial enemies – France, the United States, and China – for friendly cultural exchanges.

Currently, the effort is both inward, with the continuing development of dramas that explore the problems relevant to a rapidly changing society – such as the repercussions of people displaced by years of war, the break-up of families, and the plight of jobless youth – and also outward, in that most dramatists are very hungry for exchange with foreign colleagues, and to find out about new scripts and performing techniques. New texts, whether domestic or foreign, are strongly desired, since the few practising playwrights cannot supply all the numerous troupes now clamouring for new material.

Dramatists are not in the post-colonial position of resisting outside influence, because for so long they have been isolated and regimented by their internal politics. They are well aware that foreign texts which might stimulate them as individual artists might not play to their audiences or pass government muster. Still, they are now in the stage of opening up, possessing great and urgent curiosity – not to succumb to western trends, but to interact, and be recognized and engaged internationally.

Notes

1. In 1986, when *doi moi* was initially implemented, the law that required *cai luong* actors to be contracted to one company was repealed – creating havoc when actors threatened to walk out just before a performance to coerce producers to pay them more. This remains a problem and troupes often have to make last-minute changes.

2. My appreciation to Hanoi resident Barbara Cohen for pointing this out.

3. The term *tuong* is now commonly used to mean 'a play' rather than specifically a *tuong* performance. *Tuong*, as a specific form of classical theatre, is the state-authorized official name used alike by the present government, the former Confucian mandarins, and the intelligentsia at large. It is current, however, primarily in the North and Central parts of the country. *Hat boi* is the term used in the South for the same style of classical theatre.

4. Vietnam has always had male and female actors together on stage, and there was little cross-gendered performance. Many *cheo* plays have a strong female slant, and when *tuong* was adapted from Chinese dramas, women performed the female roles. The only time that men played female roles was at the beginning of the twentieth century, for the early *kich noi* performances, since girls from respectable families were not to be seen on stage. Occasionally, *cheo* actresses would play the roles but other women soon took over.

5. In 1997, playwright and *cheo* performer Nguyen Thi Hong Ngat was preparing a *cheo* play with director Pham Thi Thanh, but said she would no longer write *cheo*, since writing the verse was too time-consuming, and the performances did not attract large enough audiences. Spoken dramas were much easier, she said, and more popular.

6. Most of the established dramatists and teachers at the two national Institutes of Theatre and Cinema trained in the former USSR and Soviet bloc countries.

7. There does not seem to be any official vetting of texts except when troupes apply for government money, but troupes are required to give a preview performance to allow censors any last-minute changes. Overt sexuality and anti-communism are both forbidden. Performances of a play based on André Gide's *Pastoral Symphony* were banned because of Gide's anti-communist stance. Another play, based on the classical Chinese tale *The Mustard-Seed Dream*, was stopped after fifty performances for the reason that it was 'outside Marxism'.

8. Tran Huu Trang was a famous *cai luong* playwright through the 1930s to 1960s. In 1960, he founded the South Vietnam National Front for Liberation and also became president of the Liberation Association for Culture and Arts. He was killed during a US air raid in 1966, and in 1975 his name was given to the biggest *cai luong* company in Ho Chi Minh City (Huy Dzung, p. 81-2).

9. The Tran Huu Trang troupe which regularly performs out of the Hung Dao theatre recently received an award of recognition by the city. Gangs operating in the area were frightening off patrons and the troupe conducted talks with the gangs directly and got them to desist, revitalizing the whole neighbourhood.

10. During the American War and the following two decades, foreign dramas continued to be staged both in the North and the South: 'While US imperialists bombed the North, Hanoi theatre performed Arthur Miller's *All My Sons* as well as *Oedipus, The Lark, Ghosts, Turandot,* and *Sakuntala'* (Nguyen Duc Loc, p. 87). Playwrights more contemporary than Miller and Williams have not received much exposure. Students in the foreign language departments at the universities read Pirandello and Beckett, but do not expect to see them staged. An English translation of Thich Nhat Hanh's *The Path of Return Continues the Journey* was published in 1972 by Hoa Binh Press. There are French translations of some *tuong* scripts, and Russian translations of modern Vietnamese playscripts by authors who are well known within Vietnam.

11. Apartment 5B, Vo Van Tan in Ho Chi Minh City is the home of Cau Lac Bo San Khau The Nghiem. The group is referred to as a 'club' because it serves as a union for its members, supporting them when they are out of work, and providing pensions and health-care benefits. Currently about one hundred actors, directors, and playwrights belong. Hanoi has many mini-theatre productions but no one central place for their regular performance.

12. However, some new plays still befuddle the audience. An experimental piece called *Strange Story* (*Chuyen La*) by Le Duy Hang (the Vice-President of the Association of Arts and Literature in Ho Chi Minh City) was bizarre and convoluted, leaving the audience completely confused as to what it was supposed to convey, and yet people still enjoyed the moments of comedy and melodrama.

13. There are three melodic modes in *cai luong* singing: *xuan* (happiness); *ai* (sadness); *oan* (more sorrowful than sadness, and also including feelings of reproach and complaint). Vong Co is in the *oan* mode. It originally began with four stanzas, but this has been extended to eight, sixteen, and thirty-two. Although 'Vong co' is the most popular lament, this has not prevented it from being taken to extremes and evolving into self-parody. As drama reporter Phu My Lien remarks, some singers have become famous singing comic versions of it.

14. One seasoned actor, Viet Anh, appears in many of the mini-theatre productions in Ho Chi Minh City. He is an excellent character actor, showing restraint in the sentimental scenes and marvellous timing in the comic scenes. Commenting on the evident differences between northern and southern styles of acting, Tran Minh Ngoc acknowledged that the North tends to be more stylized and formal while the South is more natural. Barbara Cohen attributes the differences to historical influences: 'To this day, people of the south, influenced by Hindu and Polynesian cultures, seem generally more easy-going and flexible, while northerners are more bound by Chinese-influenced Confucian thinking and ritualistic deference to authority' (Cohen, p. 45).

15. In 1996, a Vietnamese playwright from Australia, who had written a play about the Vietnamese community and its problems in a white majority culture, was trying to get it produced in Vietnam but was not receiving any interest from local dramatists.

16. The Association is a non-governmental organization whose members qualify by the quantity and quality of their work. It sponsors playwriting contests, publications and exhibitions (Dang, 1996).

17. *The Charcoal Stove* (*Cai bep lo*), a spoken drama, was premiering in Ho Chi Minh City in 1997 for the city-sponsored festival at Tet and presented the obverse

side of *The House with No Men*, depicting a factory compound with no women. A baby is left among the male workers, who all adopt the child. They are tyrannized by their boss who forbids them wine, women, and freedom, but who himself develops an affection for the child, and through a series of coincidences discovers it is the child of his long-lost daughter. The happy family reunion also results in him becoming a decent fellow towards his employees.

18. One of the first *cai luong* was based on *Luc Van Tieu*, a popular verse novel written by Nguyen Dinh Chieu, a southern writer. After 1954, the novel was required reading material for schoolchildren. Since most literature was written by northerners, and the new government wanted an equal selection from all parts of the country, *Luc Van Tieu* was chosen to represent the South.

19. Historical *cai luong* seem to be more popular in the countryside, while those in contemporary dress are favored by urban audiences. In both cases, old melodies are used; it is too expensive for most troupes to commission new music.

20. Although *cai luong* plays tend to have weepy endings, special plays with happy endings are prepared for performances during and around Tet, when people prefer less dolorous entertainments. *Cai luong* companies are allowed to produce only four new plays a year; this, Nguyen Thi Minh Ngoc says, makes it difficult to earn enough to keep the company going.

21. *Thunderstorm* (*Leiyu*) was the most significant modern spoken drama (*huaju*) in China. Since its premiere in 1935, it has continued to exert an influence in China and the region. In the early 1990s, various productions of the play – both *cai luong* and *kich noi* – were being performed all over Vietnam, and were very popularly received.

References

Ai Nhu, 1997. Interview with the author, Ho Chi Minh City, Vietnam, 29 January.

Bowers, Fabion, 1960. *Theatre in the East: a Survey of Asian Dance and Drama* (New York: Grove Press), p. 303-7.

Brandon, James, 1993. 'Vietnam', in *The Cambridge Guide to Asian Theatre* (Cambridge: Cambridge University Press).

——, 1967. *Theatre in Southeast Asia* (Cambridge: Harvard University Press), p. 245-50.

Buttinger, Joseph, 1968. *Vietnam: a Political History* (New York: Praeger Publishers).

Cohen, Barbara, 1990. *The Vietnam Guide Book* (New York: Harper and Row).

Dang Tran Can, 1996-97. Interview with the author, Hanoi, Vietnam, 13-14 February.

Do Muoi, 1996. 'The Unofficial Translation of the Main Body of the Address Made by General Secretary Do Muoi at the Opening of the Eighth National Congress of Communist Party of Vietnam', *Vietnam News*, 29 June.

Hoang Kieu, 1987. '*Cheo*: a Vietnamese Folk Stage and Singing Theatre', in *Vietnam Social Sciences* (Hanoi: Committee for Social Sciences), p. 28-34.

Hoang To Mai, 1997. Interview with the author, Hanoi, Vietnam, 10 February.

Hoefer, Hans, 1991. *Vietnam: Insight Guides* (Hong Kong: APA Publications), p. 127-32.

Huy Dzung, 1987. 'Tran Huu Trang and Cai Luong in the South', *Vietnamese Studies*, New Series, XVII, p. 76-86.

Huy Thinh, 1996. 'Can We Hope For More Attractive Films?', *Vietnam Courier*, February, p. 11-17.

Janaczewska, Noelle, 1994. 'They're Dancing the Lambada in Hanoi', *Australasian Drama Studies*, No. 25, p. 152-65.

Le Hong Ly, 1996. Interview with the author and later correspondence, Hanoi, Vietnam, 9 February.

Le Minh Ly, 1996. 'Cultural Education Should Be Targeted', *Vietnam News*, July, p. 1.

Ly Khac Cung, 1996-97. Interviews with the author, Hanoi, Vietnam, 10-12 February.

Mackerras, Colin, 1987. 'Theatre in Vietnam', *Asian Theatre Journal*, IV, No. 1, p. 1-28.

Mettienen, Jukka, 1993. *Classical Dance and Theatre in South-East Asia* (Oxford: Oxford University Press), p. 162-8.

Ngo Thao, 1987. 'The Problems of Kich Noi at Present', *Vietnam Social Sciences* (Hanoi: Committee for Social Sciences), p. 66-71.

Ngoc Linh, 1993. *The House With No Men* (*Ngoi nah khong co dan ong*) (Hanoi: Nha xuat ban san khau).

Nguyen Duc Loc, 1987. 'Vietnamese Theatre and its Friends', *Vietnam Social Science* (Hanoi: Committee for Social Sciences), p. 83-7.

Nguyen Thi Hong Ngat, 1997. Interview with the author, Hanoi, Vietnam, 9 February.

Nguyen Thi Minh Ngoc, 1996-97. Interviews with the author, Ho Chi Minh City, Vietnam, 25 January-6 February.

Pham Thi Thanh, 1996-97. Interviews with the author, Hanoi, Vietnam, 12-15 February.

Pham Van Ty, 1996. Interview with the author, Hanoi, Vietnam, 9 February.

Phu My Lien, 1996-97. Interviews with the author and later correspondence, Ho Chi Minh City, Vietnam, 5-6 February.

Tat Thang, 1987. 'Tuong: the Art of the Heroes with a Noble Ideal', *Vietnam Social Sciences* (Hanoi: Committee for Social Sciences), p. 23-27.

Thanh Minh, 1996. 'Low-Budget Films out of Fashion', *Vietnam News*, 2 February.

The Gioi Publishers (no author), 1995. *Vietnam* (Hanoi: The Gioi Publishers).

To Ngoc Tranh, 1996. Interview with the author and later correspondence, Hanoi, Vietnam, 10 February.

Tran Minh Ngoc, 1996-97. Interviews with the author, Hanoi, Vietnam, 5-7 February.

Tran Van Khe, 1996. Correspondence with the author, 10 April.

Tu Luong, 1987. '*Cai luong*: a Theatre in Rapid Development', *Vietnam Social Sciences* (Hanoi: Committee for Social Sciences), p. 56-65.

Jane Plastow

The Eritrea Community-Based Theatre Project

Following Jane Plastow's contextual history of Eritrean theatre in NTQ50, Paul Warwick gave an account in the following issue of its previously undocumented role during the thirty-year Eritrean struggle for independence, describing the efforts of the freedom fighters to create theatre for the first time in a rural context. The Eritrean People's Liberation Front not only deployed theatre as a propaganda weapon, but also recognized its value as an agent for educating the people in matters ranging from women's rights to the benefits of modern medicine and farming methods: and with victory came measures further to stimulate the growth and development of theatre as part of Eritrean culture. Jane Plastow, in this third and concluding article, takes up the story with the invitation issued by the new government to her and her colleagues to initiate the 'Eritrea Community-Based Theatre Project', in an attempt both to widen the perspectives of Eritrean actors and to draw upon all relevant traditions, African and European, in developing a popular but distinctive theatre for the people. In addition to her role as director of the project, Jane Plastow is a lecturer at Leeds University, having worked in theatre for some years in a number of other African nations.

THE ERITREA Community-Based Theatre Project came into being as the result of a chance meeting between the then head of the Eritrean Division of Culture, Alemseged Tesfai, and myself, held in Addis Ababa, Ethiopia, in the spring of 1992. Alemseged was looking for ways to build up a national theatre culture in the aftermath of Africa's longest war this century – the thirty-year struggle of the Eritrean people to win their independence from the brutally oppressive Ethiopian colonization, as described by Paul Warwick and myself in earlier articles in *New Theatre Quarterly.*

A mutual Ethiopian friend introduced us, and the result was an invitation to Eritrea to discuss possible ways forward for indigenous theatre. Three years later a group of British theatre workers – Mary Boyle, Oliver Fox, Paul Warwick, myself, my four-year-old son, and a friend I had recruited to act as his nanny – flew to Eritrea in July 1995 to run a three-month intensive theatre training programme with 57 Eritrean trainees.

It is essential to understand that Eritrea had been effectively cut off from the outside world for thirty years. The only country whose culture Eritreans had any regular access to during that time was Ethiopia, and Ethiopia was waging a genocidal war aimed at eradicating Eritrean art, Eritrean voices, and ultimately the Eritrean people. None of the trainees we worked with had ever had access to a book about theatre. None of them had any idea that there might be different forms and styles of producing theatre. None of them had ever received any formal actor training.

Eritrean theatre was sharply divided between the traditional performance arts, which for all nine of the country's ethnic groups were music, song, and dance-based, and drama which was dialogue-dominated and aspired to naturalism. Drama, as in most of Africa, was a colonial import from Eritrea's succession of colonizers – the Italians, the British, and the Ethiopians.

Historically, many African nations went through a period where colonial ideas of drama were introduced as superior to and separate from the traditional performance modes, but in most nations as nationalist agendas developed, and through exchange of ideas and performance tours, traditional and imported theatre forms have increasingly been integrated and syncretized. In Ethiopia and Eritrea this process had never happened: drama was largely an elite, urban tool for propaganda or escapist comedy and romance, usually produced in tandem with the performance of traditional and modern music and song.

The Project and its Precedents

When Eritrea gained its independence in May 1991, Alemseged Tesfai was given the task of developing a cultural policy. The intention of the new government was to promote a wide range of arts and to encourage an arts establishment independent of state control or support. But the authorities were also aware that Eritrean theatre was undeveloped and that training and new ideas needed to be introduced. When I met Alemseged he was looking at Ethiopian theatre models with a view to developing a national theatre along Ethiopian lines.

In the course of our meetings we came to discuss community and development theatre initiatives in other parts of Africa, an area in which I had been working and researching for a number of years. Although during the liberation struggle the Eritrean Peoples' Liberation Front (EPLF) had sought to use theatre in creative and relevant ways, the concept of a community-based theatre as developed in other parts of Africa was unknown in Eritrea. The upshot of our discussions was that I was invited to visit Eritrea to discuss the possibility of developing a community-based theatre project.

That visit took place in the Easter vacation of 1993, and ended only a week before the referendum supervised by the UN which showed over 99 per cent of the people in favour of becoming an independent state – so the atmosphere was vibrant with optimism. I was chaperoned through an intensive schedule of watching EPLF cultural videos, seeing local amateur plays, running theatre workshops using EPLF actors – and meeting after meeting, ranging from discussions with the Minister of Information to less formal talks with performers and study groups. Although there was obviously so much to be done in devastated Eritrea that I kept wanting to apologise for taking up people's time with such a 'luxury' as debates about theatre, I was assured that everyone placed a great importance on the development of their national culture and on finding ways of giving a voice to people whose language, art forms, and freedom of expression had been so strongly denied by the Ethiopian oppressors. Eritrea was crying out for new ideas, and wanted to build a knowledge base from which to choose its way forward.

Back in England, on the basis of our discussions, I drew up a project proposal for the Eritrea Community-Based Theatre Project which was accepted and became the basis for the 1995 work. The philosophy of the project was not new to Africa: it was based on my own work, observations, and research with community, popular, and development theatre practice in various African countries, and drew most heavily on work in Zimbabwe.

Here, as in Eritrea, performance work had played an important role in politicizing people about the liberation struggle of the 1970s. Consequently Zimbabweans and left-wing theatre practitioners from South Africa, Zambia, and Kenya had worked together to develop a vibrant community-oriented theatre movement which encompassed a wide variety of modes of working and styles of theatre, offering workshops and eventually an independent organizing body, ZACT – the Zimbabwe Association of Community Theatres.

ZACT was not a trouble-free zone. There had been personality clashes and differences of group philosophies. More significantly, the initially supportive government had come to have increasing reservations about a movement which often criticized the state on stage. But ZACT's desire to empower, to train, and to support theatre groups in an undoctrinaire manner, building on the people's own culture and experiences as a starting point, has proved itself as a viable way of developing a dynamic theatre movement in Zimbabwe.

I also drew heavily on the ideas of Ngugi wa Thiong'o. It was fortunate that in Eritrea language could never be the issue it was for Ngugi. Eritrean plays had almost always been put on in local languages, but the philosophy of empowerment behind Ngugi's work in Kamiriithu coincided strongly with the way Eritrea now wanted to develop her own culture. Finally, I was able to utilize my own critical studies of Ethiopian theatre, which has many similarities with Eritrean drama.

EPLF cultural troupes had gone some way towards trying to broaden the relevance of Eritrean drama, and on a few occasions had experimented with integrating indigenous performance modes with drama, but this was not looked on as 'proper' theatre. In the urban areas, and particularly in Asmara (which had remained under Ethiopian control until the end of the war), drama remained utterly divided from indigenous performance forms.

The playwright, as in Ethiopia, was seen as all-important in serious drama, with actors used predominantly as mouthpieces for his (invariably his) words. In comedy there was a more improvisational tradition, but urban comedy was almost always reactionary in subject-matter and was not seen as an appropriate genre for the discussion of serious themes. Eritrean theatre had long been forbidden to deal with political issues, so the numerous amateur groups tended to put on a diet of romances and comedies, which filled the theatres only with urban youth who came to enjoy a diet of uncritical escapism.

The intention of the Eritrea Community-Based Theatre Project was to work with a wide variety of trainees, including EPLF cultural troupes, urban amateur groups, youth associations, and the teaching profession, and drawing on actors, playwrights, musicians, singers, and dancers to try to encourage a syncretized theatre which could work with indigenous and relevant foreign concepts of performance to make issue-based theatre within an aesthetic which, although flexible, would be distinctively Eritrean and able to speak to all Eritreans, with a particular emphasis on the majority of the rural peasantry.

The First Week

When we first arrived in Asmara we knew where we wanted to be heading, but we deliberately had no fixed plan about how to get there. We had all spent time reading about the Eritrean struggle, and had undertaken a crash introduction to Tigrinya, the language amongst Eritrea's nine indigenous languages which is most widely spoken in the area around Asmara. But our knowledge was pretty basic.

Ultimately we were to run three groups of trainees, two in Asmara and one in Keren, a town of some 50,000 people ninety kilometres to the west of the capital. We also brought in trainees from the port of Massawa and from some smaller towns around Asmara. This was important because we did not want our efforts to be limited to the capital. It has happened so often in Africa that training becomes concentrated in the capital, thus encouraging an influx from the rest of the country and an imbalance in resources and opportunities.

Asmara is a beautiful city, built by the Italians with wide palm-lined main streets, suburbs of Mediterranean-style villas, and a host of small bars. It is also grossly overcrowded, with the mass of the people crammed into shanty town shacks in what was originally intended as the Eritrean workers' end of town. We were to work from Cinema Asmara, an extraordinarily dilapidated but beautiful old building which had been built by the Italians as an Opera House. However, it had an evil smell, due to the failing drainage system, very dim lighting, and an enormously high and narrow stage which worked against the integrated nature of the work we were trying to undertake. We decided most of the time to use the much more open, light spaces of the foyer and a large upstairs room.

For the first week, in order to familiarize ourselves with the group and with each other, we all worked together with just one group of seventeen trainees, varying in age

Warm-up session in the theatre in Asmara.

from 16 to 53. Some had been full-time theatre or traditional arts workers with the EPLF groups, but more than half were amateurs who were otherwise students, teachers, tailors, farmers, shop-workers, or unemployed.

What was most striking in this first week was that our trainees were desperate for knowledge of how theatre worked in other places. What they wanted from us was to be taught about theatre – and mostly about acting. They saw us as acting teachers who would basically show them how to be better naturalistic actors – whereas we wanted to be empowerers working with indigenous traditions and talking about alternative ways of making theatre. These differences of approach required a lot of talking through, the core problem being a lack of a conception that there *could* be alternative ways of making theatre.

The Working Routine

After our first day's work the training group gathered for what became nightly planning sessions. We decided that the best way to satisfy an obvious craving for hard concepts and a wider theatre vocabulary, while demonstrating that theatre could come in many interesting forms, was to spend our first month looking at the work of practitioners whose ideas of theatre might be relevant to the Eritrean situation. While deciding to concentrate on Boal and Brecht, and on African popular theatre models as exemplified by Ngugi wa Thiong'o, we also looked at Stanislavsky – not because we particularly wanted to promote naturalism, but because, although our trainees had never heard his name, naturalism was what they believed theatre to be, and we wanted them therefore to have some idea of his philosophy and training techniques.

We could only give a week to each practitioner, during which we could barely introduce the concepts we wanted to work with. But we hoped this would encourage trainees to begin to think about the range of theatrical alternatives open to them and how they could be applied in a local context. To supplement practical teaching, and at the students' request, we also prepared handouts in English and Tigrinya on the practitioners we studied.

A mode of working quickly emerged. Workshops ran from Monday to Saturday from eight to one o'clock, with a short coffee break in the middle. Every day began with a warm-up session which included physical and voice work, and built up a repertoire of theatre games. At first many students found these quite funny, but we felt this basic work was very important: it brought the disparate group together, and also made actors recognize their bodies as tools, indigenous drama having tended to be very static. These warm-up sessions also allowed us to get the students to lead with work on local songs and dances, which moved control from us to them and brought indigenous performance techniques into the work from an early stage.

The emphasis each week was on practical work. We moved from exercises based on the work of the practitioner in question towards small presentations attempting to deal with Eritrean issues chosen by trainees, explored through the theatrical methods of the practitioner being studied. However, we knew there would have to be a lot of talking and discussion, and there was.

Each week we had one formal seminar-cum-lecture session, but this proved to be a slow process. Because our Tigrinya was so limited we had to work through interpreter-members who were attached to each group. This meant all discussion and explanation had to go back and forth between the two languages. Discussions were often intense and at times fairly heated, both between trainers and trainees and among the trainees themselves. Beyond the formal discussion sessions, the practical workshops also involved a lot of talking, simply because almost everything we did was new to the people we were working with, both practically and in terms of theatre philosophy.

The discussions were fascinating, time and time again throwing up the division between the mostly civilian and formally educated urban students – who had difficulty in valuing anything other than a hierarchical and playwright-led 'art' theatre – and the fighters, who were much more receptive to a more democratic mode of working and who wanted to create a theatre relevant to ordinary Eritreans. Winning the participants over to new philosophies of theatre was a gradual process, and it was really only in the practice of the final tour, undertaken at the end of the programme, that the hard core of intellectual resisters became convinced of the potential for a community-based theatre.

Relevance and Irrelevance of Models

The other main focus for discussion was when people said 'this is not in our culture', usually as a reason for not trying something new. This could refer either to a mode of working, as in Boalian forum theatre, or to issues being performed – often those which centred around women's liberation. This was sensitive ground. The question as to whether we were merely cultural imperialists in a new guise was one of which we were acutely aware – though fortunately Eritrean national self-confidence runs so high that discussions about these issues could be fairly robust.

I have never been in an African country where race was less of an issue. The process of the struggle had given people an extremely sophisticated ability to differentiate between issues of race and issues of oppression. Ultimately this meant we could ask people to try out new ideas even when they were difficult for them, because they were happy to argue out problems and knew that it would be their choice as to what was taken up and what was not in the long run.

The most intriguing aspect of the Boal week was that it became clear that his ideas could have only a limited application in Eritrea – simply because most people, in particular the fighters, did not feel remotely oppressed. And how do you work with a concept of 'Theatre of the Oppressed' in a country where most people do not believe oppression exists? The belief that the government really belonged to the people was extraordinary to those of us coming from a western environment. Students lived in considerable poverty amidst the many problems of their war-devastated country, yet their only (and quite genuine) solution to most of the problems on which we focused was simply 'We must work harder.'

After the first week we moved on and opened other project groups – which was harder for us as we no longer had the luxury of working off each other. Mary Boyle was the most isolated here as she was primarily responsible for the Keren group ninety kilometres away, and even getting a phone link between the towns could take hours, only to find that the line was often so bad as to be almost useless.

For me the most interesting work in this first section was the week spent looking at African theatre models. I ran this with each group in turn, since I was the Africanist and because we wanted to swop staff around in order to give trainees access to different approaches. Most trainees had never considered that, separately from the content of a theatrical performance, the *style* of its production might be oppressive. A few had heard of Ngugi, but they had little knowledge of how culture had been used as a tool of oppression by the succession of Eritrea's colonists. The practical work that came out of the groups was also exciting. For the first time we were really bringing in the performance traditions of Eritrea, and the work began to take on an urgency and energy that came with a belief in the value of what the trainees were doing.

By the end of that month we all felt real changes were taking place. Energy was most important in this. Because actors were used simply to doing as they were told, the style of acting had initially been very slow. Actors traditionally did not start to perform until they were well on stage. They tended to look out front all the time, and action itself counted far less than words. Moreover, most of our female participants were very reluctant to push themselves forward, and had considerable problems making themselves heard. All the groups were short on women members. In Asmara all the women were fighters, and in Keren all were extremely young. Acting is not considered at all a respectable activity for older civilian women, in spite of the emphasis the social revolution has placed on women's issues.

Much of our work concentrated on getting groups to work as ensembles, and on showing (as opposed to merely talking about) the issues in question. Such notions may sound basic, but they were truly revolutionary in Eritrea. Our other major problem lay in persuading trainees to experiment with ways of improvising scenes. The tendency was to take an idea, find a way to perform it, and after ten minutes say the work was done. Encouraging people to look at a performance question from different angles was a major aspect of our work.

The whole education system as it had been run under Ethiopian occupation was highly authoritarian, as also was traditional Eritrean society. Debate and experiment had been strongly repressed, and, despite the more open attitude among the fighters, even here people were unused to working in an improvisational manner, and were lacking in confidence about playing with new theatrical ideas.

The Second Stage

Our second month was to be devoted to Eritrean theatre forms. Each group had a few expert musicians, singers, and dancers, and we wanted them to lead the others in order to see how these elements could be brought into our theatre work. This nearly provoked a mini-mutiny. A number of participants thought we had run out of ideas and were simply passing the buck. Others said they could have done work like this without us, and they wanted more western theory instead – which was rather depressing, since we had spent so much time talking about the idea behind integrating traditional and modern theatre forms.

I felt strongly that a vocal minority still saw the people's performance forms as inferior. Fortunately others strongly supported the work, and later several trainees told me they realized how little they knew of their own traditions, and that on their own they would never have spent time looking at such performance modes.

For us this work was fascinating, because we got to see the operation of Eritrean performance styles. It was also extremely useful in making Eritreans the leaders, particularly those – such as traditional musicians and dancers – whose status was fairly low with some of the urban, educated students. It was in this area that Ollie Fox, our multi-skilled musician, took the lead in working with the Eritrean musicians, though sometimes he found this very hard, since Eritrean music has close affinities with Arab music, and is often very repetitive in both content and form.

It seemed to all of us that although Eritrean cultural traditions were strong they were also thin. The nation has acquired something of a siege mentality and lacks the energy and vibrancy that comes from cultural cross-fertilization. New forms, modern music, and colonial drama techniques had been taken on in urban areas, but traditional performance forms had tended to become closed in on themselves, and to us there seemed a lack of creativity because nothing new had been added to the mix for so long.

This notion was reinforced when we came to work on folk tales. Story-telling is very strong in many parts of Africa, and is often very much part of the indigenous performance culture – but in Eritrea some people obviously felt rather insulted at being required to work on such 'childish' material. The stories were also thin on the ground. Although there were a number of anthropomorphic tales and of religiously derived stories, what amazed me was that none of the groups could come up with a story which involved magic, fantasy, or a vision of a non-literal universe. Eventually trainees made up and workshopped some very imaginative stories of their own: but again the repression of church and society, and the consequences of war and isolation, seem to have had a strangling effect on people's natural creativity.

Developing the Performances

The progress of an intensive three-month programme is difficult to evaluate when you are in the midst of it. But two-thirds of the way through we could see considerable developments in the way the students were working. The ability to work as a cohesive ensemble had advanced enormously, with many of the quieter members of the groups gaining the confidence to express ideas and suggest ways of putting them into practice. The visual, performative sense had also become quite startlingly sharper. All of our trainees had lived through some extremely dramatic times, and they produced images of struggle, brutality, torture, and heroism which were shocking because of their immediacy and because we knew they had actually been experienced.

Our intention in the final month of the training programme was for each group to work towards a devised performance which would not look back to the struggle but forwards to the reconstruction of Eritrea. We therefore started by asking students to come up with issues which they felt were important to Eritrea at the present time. Each student came up with his or her own ideas, and these were then discussed before a short-list was brought to each of the project groups for final selection.

The issues which came top of the lists were housing, reconciliation of the various groups within Eritrean society in the post-struggle context, education (especially for girls, linked to women's rights in general), AIDS, maintaining the family as a strong unit, land redistribution, and general health issues.

The final three plays all dealt with aspects of women's rights, and particularly with the need for women to have access to educational opportunities – the main thrust of the Keren play. One of the Asmara groups chose to focus on understanding AIDS, the other on land issues – who should be given land in a society where families are divided between fighters, returning refugees, and urban dwellers, some of whom made money out of working with the Ethiopians.

After agreeing on the issues to be dealt with in the plays, trainees went out in small groups to carry out research. This involved interviews with relevant government bodies and NGOs, and interviewing people affected by the issues in question. Thus far the work had all been in the students' hands: but, since we now had only two weeks to produce our plays, coming up with an outline plot as an ensemble was felt to be too difficult, and the trainers for each group therefore wrote a broad outline for their play which was discussed and modified by the students according to how they felt it could work credibly within an Eritrean context.

The actual improvisations of the plays came out of two weeks of extremely hard work from all involved. Some songs and dances – which played a crucial part in all the plays – were indigenous and were taught to the others by those who knew them best. Other songs and poems – for poetry is an important part of this rhetorical culture – were written by those in the group who were interested and in some cases had already worked as playwrights, while new music was composed by other students.

The plays were devised, again amidst constant discussion, with a mixture of supervision and direction from the trainers – our constant emphasis being on maintaining energy levels, pace, and dramatic tension. The plays were intended to be taken primarily to rural areas where little, if any, theatre had ever been seen, and it was vital that not only should the plays be made accessible through the integration of indigenous performance modes, but also that they should hold and involve the audience through both their style and content. The idea was that in each venue we would perform two of the three plays each of about an hour in length.

To make our plays we drew mostly on other African community theatre models, but also quite heavily on Brechtian ideas. All the plays had a loosely epic format with short scenes requiring the audience to evaluate different aspects of the issues being discussed. Two used narration techniques, and two made no attempt to present an enclosed world of the play but interacted directly with the audience. Perhaps what proved most novel was the mixing of genres, for the juxtaposition of the comic and the tragic – combined with direct address to the audience – had been unheard of in Eritrea.

Because very few places have electricity in Eritrea we would take a generator and two floodlights, but that was the extent of the technology involved, and most of the props and costumes were either begged or borrowed. The plays were deliberately 'low tec' not only because we wanted them not to appear alien to rural audiences, but also because we hoped these audiences might feel empowered to do something similar.

Going on Tour

By this time all of the trainers were nearing exhaustion. Most of us had been ill from a new malaria drug which had strong side effects until we all abandoned it. My son had had a dose of acute food poisoning in Keren, and Ollie Fox had attracted a bug which led to the revival of a chronic bowel condition. Work was further interrupted by the nanny deciding to get married with the full panoply of Orthodox ritual.

For the tour Solomon Tsehaye (the new head of cultural affairs) and I had plotted what we hoped would be a representative itinerary within easy reach of Asmara. We would start off in Keren, then go on to Embardorho, a large village of some 9,000 people. Next would come a smaller rural settlement, Sala'a Daro, and we would end with the small town of Decemhare and a performance before an invited audience in Asmara itself. In Keren, Decemhare, and Asmara we would play in local halls, whilst in Embadorho and Sala'a Daro we would perfrm in the open-air in the school playing fields.

In each place Solomon and I paid visits to the local community leaders to get permission to mount the plays, and they had agreed to publicize the event. The actors simply turned up on the day in the buses we had hired. We agreed the best place to perform – when in the open air, trying to find a slope from which the audience could sit looking down at us. We then rigged up the generator and got ready to perform at around seven in the evening.

In each place a more than adequate audience at the beginning of the piece then grew and grew, watching mostly in total silence except for bursts of laughter, until in

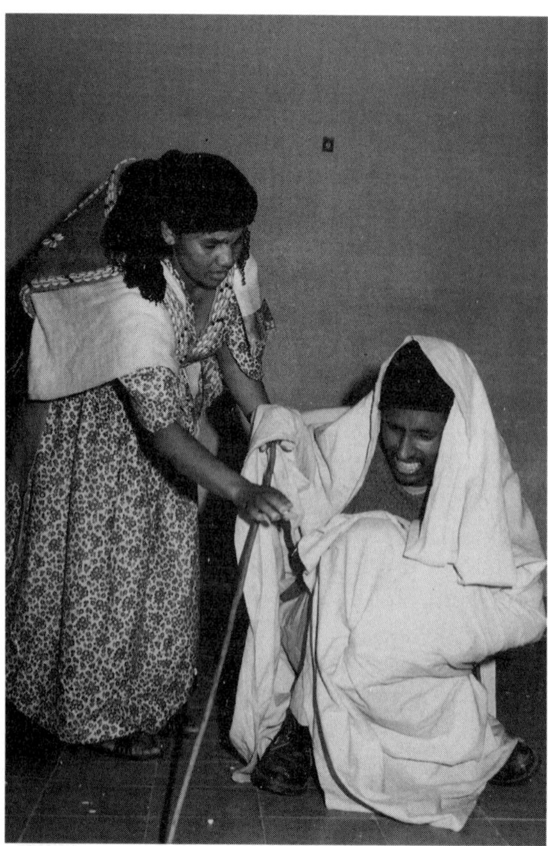

Above: abused wife and dying husband in the AIDS play in Keren. Opposite page: preparing the performing space in the school grounds at Sala'a Daro.

the open-air venues the playing space was totally encircled. Indeed, our biggest problem everywhere was simply fitting people in: in Decemhare we had to have police on the door to keep crowds back, whilst in Embadorho the play had to be stopped for a while because the pressure of a crowd of thousands kept threatening to crush those at the front.

At the end there was no applause, for this is not part of the culture, but we were never in any doubt as to the attention paid, and informal interviews with the audience carried out by actors were extremely positive. What is more, the few remaining trainees whose doubts about the aesthetic merit of our proceedings lasted right up until the tour were now finally convinced not only that this form of theatre could work, but that a peasant audience could be its worthy recipients.

The project was never intended to be a one-off endeavour, and from the earliest meetings with Alemseged we had discussed how the work could be both sustained and developed in the long term. However, when we arrived to run the training programme there were no specific plans as to what form a follow-up might take – partly because none of us knew what the end result of the course might be in terms of quality or popularity, but also because policies for the development of Eritrea are still being evolved and in many areas remain fluid.

The Follow Up

Trainees were selected because they were already involved in performance arts, and at a basic level we hoped that the skills they had acquired during the training course might be taken back into schools, amateur groups, and EPLF troupes as a new input to that work – and even while we were in Eritrea there was evidence that this was happening. The latest play by the EPLF cultural troupe thus incorporated many of the techniques we were experimenting with, while amateur groups in Keren were beginning to use new ideas about theatre. Beyond this we were asked both for lectures and handout materials from many amateur groups and schools who heard of our work from places around the country. We tried to fit in as much extra as we could, but we were not able to satisfy the sheer volume of requests for talks and information.

Secondly, Solomon and I talked from early on in the project about building up a core group of professional performers who would carry on the work we had started, both in taking theatre out to the rural areas and in passing on training to villages, so that a network of community groups with relevant skills could be built up. Sixteen people have duly formed a Community-Based Theatre Group, and this has recently completed its first two-month tour of the Tigrinya-speaking areas of Eritrea.

The group toured two plays – *Land*, which had been devised during the training programme, and *Marriage*, which looks at

issues of dowry payment, virginity, and the abuse which young brides can suffer. The group has toured with local transport, occasionally trekking with pack camels to the remoter villages, and estimates to have reached around 90,000 people in the course of the tour. The response has been hugely enthusiastic, as I saw when I returned to Eritrea at Easter 1996, and funding has now been secured from a number of agencies which will keep the group employed for at least the coming year with a mixture of theatre touring and training projects.

Further training projects have also taken place or been projected. In the late summer of 1996 a theatre-in-education training course for 25 primary school teachers was given by two trainers from England – Paul Warwick, who was our researcher on the first trip, and Gail McIntyre, who is an expert in the area and runs the schools programme at the West Yorkshire Playhouse in Leeds.

In the summer of 1997 a two-pronged training course is planned. A basic course will be run for Tigre-speaking people, as our aim is to extend possibilities to as many language groups as possible, whilst the Tigrinya professional group will work in two villages with experienced leaders of popular theatre programmes from other African countries, aiming at the creation of community theatre with the people of those villages. This training we hope will complete the process of turning trainees into trainers, and increase their independence from outside tutelage.

In the medium term Eritrea wants to set up an arts college, and to open up theatre training opportunities to people from other language groups. The need immediately is for Eritreans to get sufficient training to develop a dynamic nationwide theatre network. Given the extraordinary achievements of the liberation struggle and the commitment of so many of the Eritreans we met to building their nation, there are good grounds for optimism. For all the trainers, working in Eritrea was an exhausting and most humbling honour for which we are deeply grateful.

NTQ Book Reviews

edited by Maggie Gale

Theatre History to 1900

Janet Todd, ed.
Aphra Behn Studies
Cambridge: Cambridge University Press, 1996.
ISBN 0-521-47169-9.

Aimed at students of seventeenth-century literature, and in particular at those interested in
women's writing, Janet Todd's volume collects
fifteen articles representing current Behn studies.
Divided into three main sections (plays, poems,
and fiction) and with a brief final section on new
work on Behn's biography, this book is essential
reading for the Behn devotee. As well as indicating the breadth of Behn's literary output, however, this book also demonstrates the limitations
of current Behn scholarship. This is especially clear
in the 'plays' section, where three of five articles
focus on the politics of the plays and only one is
concerned directly with drama as performance.

The emphasis on politics, and in particular
on the Popish plot, is central in Susan Owen's
exploration of the sexual politics engendered by
Toryism, in Alison Shell's demonstration of
coded Catholicism in *The Feign'd Curtezans*, and
in Ros Ballaster's work on artifice. Ballaster's is a
subtle exposition of the connections between
'real' and 'fictional' intrigues, and in teasing out
the resonances of fiction, fraud, and femininity
she makes good and suggestive use of a non-
dramatic text, Elizabeth Cellier's *Malice Defeated*.
Alison Shell's argument raises the interesting
possibility of Behn's use of 'Catholic camp' – 'a
combination of elaborate secrecy, wit, implied
revelrous misbehaviour, and cautious proselyti-
zation'. And Jane Spencer's work on the stage
history of *The Rover* and on the details of adaptation indicates that behind eighteenth-century
attacks on Behn lay a continuing though changing popularity.

The problem with this book's treatment of
Behn as playwright, however, is pinpointed by
Alison Shell. She is alive to the materiality of the
printed object which juxtaposes dedication, pro-
logue, and playtext, and remarks: 'This insight,
of course, is available only to the reader', later
insisting that 'the interpretative luxury afforded
by the printed page must not be forgotten'. Any
understanding of drama as performance, here
raised in passing, eludes several of the other
contributors completely; and, sadly, the one
article claiming to deal with performance – Dawn

Lewcock's discussion of visual effects – is by far
the weakest. Badly written and stating the plod-
dingly obvious, it is a dire warning of what can
happen when plays are analyzed by people with
computers. This is, then, primarily a volume of
literary and textual criticism: isn't it time for
practitioners to have a say?

MAUREEN BELL

Derek Hughes
English Drama, 1660-1700
Oxford: Clarendon Press, 1996. 503 p.
ISBN 0-198-11974-7.

This is a fascinating and sometimes frustrating
book. Derek Hughes's encyclopedic knowledge
(he discusses over four hundred plays) allows
him to make illuminating connections between
plays great and small. To structure the work, he
focuses on the relation of plots and themes,
examining the role of the stranger, the instability
of social hierarchy, or the impact of the gay
couple on comedy. His opening chapter sets out
some of the key ideas contested during the
period, and the plays are discussed in their
topical, social, and political context.

But Hughes is at pains to point out that this
kind of survey also reveals the distinctiveness
of many plays, as his detailed readings of *The
Country Wife* or *The Man of Mode* demonstrate.
Because of the wealth of material dealt with, he
can offer only tantalising glimpses of works like
Thomas St. Serfe's intrigue play, *Tarugo's Wiles*.
Canonical authors and texts dominate the discussion, but Hughes includes Behn, whom he
treats fairly fully, as a central figure. It is his
consideration, however brief, of works by women
dramatists and lesser-known writers alongside
the 'greats' that makes this an invaluable textbook for student and researcher alike.

JANE MILLING

Adrienne Scullion, ed.
Female Playwrights of the Nineteenth Century
London: Dent, 1996. £8.99.
ISBN 0-460-87729-1.

Adrienne Scullion begins her Introduction to this
collection with the assertion that there is a perception that between Inchbald and Robins 'the
nineteenth century is all but a black hole for
plays written by women'. In recent years scholars

have retrieved many playtexts by women from this period, but few, apart from the late Ibsen-influenced New Woman plays and the suffrage drama, have found a publisher.

The great service that this volume performs is, then, to give us a group of plays that demonstrate the variety and – in most cases – popularity of women's writing for the nineteenth-century stage. The plays range from Joanna Baillie's verse drama, *The Family Legend*, to Bell and Robins's controversial realist play, *Alan's Wife*. One can always cavil about the choice of plays in any anthology, but it would have been interesting to see a pantomime and perhaps a children's drama there as well, fields in which women also made their mark.

This anthology could equally well serve as a textbook for nineteenth-century theatre, since its plays along with Scullion's Introduction illustrate how snugly these women and their work fitted within the frame of the commercial theatre. However, whilst I applaud the robust and celebratory nature of the general introduction, I think it tends to elide the problems that emerged for women dramatists with the increasing 'professionalization' of the nineteenth-century theatre, culminating in the exclusion of women from the newly founded Society of Authors in 1884. But this is a small reservation about an extremely timely and useful volume.

VIV GARDNER

Twentieth-Century Theatre

Brian Crow with Chris Banfield
An Introduction to Post-Colonial Theatre
Cambridge: Cambridge University Press, 1996.
£11.95.
ISBN 0-521-56722-X.

Helen Gilbert and Joanne Tompkins
Post Colonial Drama: Theory, Practice, Politics
London; New York: Routledge, 1996. £14.95.
ISBN 0-415-09024-5.

What is post-colonial theatre? Who are its practitioners? Is the term 'post-colonial theatre' simply another category to accommodate those theatre practitioners who, until recently, would have inhabited a marginal space on theatre history courses? In *An Introduction to Post-Colonial Theatre* Crow and Banfield offer an introduction to post-colonial theatre by recourse to major dramatists from the 'Third World and subordinated cultures within Europe and America'.

Acknowledging theatre practitioners who have borrowed from a variety of non-western cultures to enhance modes of western theatre production, the writers document and discuss the dramatic works of Derek Walcott, August Wilson, Jack Davis, Wole Soyinka, Athol Fugard, Badal Sircar, and Girish Karnad. For each practitioner the authors offer a cultural and historical context to the dramatic works, thereby highlighting the significance of both scripted and non-scripted dramas within their own cultural context. Particularly engaging is the drama of the Aboriginal history, and the dramatic works of Jack Davis, in discussing which the authors illuminate an Aboriginal reality that departs from any correct or Romantic notions of Aboriginal history and current socio-political reality.

This is an ideal book for undergraduate students who are seeking to develop a sense of dramatic text and context for theatre practices developed by indigenous writers offering (and continuing to offer) a challenge to post-colonial and neo-colonial contexts. References to Brian Friel in the conclusion dispel any notion that colonialism is of the past and post-colonialism of the present – making the issue of colonialism a contemporary as well as an historical debate.

In *Post-Colonial Drama* Helen Gilbert and Joanne Tompkins take great care to define and contextualize their usage of 'post-colonial' along with 'colonialism' and 'imperialism', drawing parallels and distinctions amongst characteristics that do not allow it to be shunted under the banner of the 'postmodern'. Discarding any easy definitions, the authors embark on a questioning and critique of 'difference' as a social, cultural, historical, and political reality within previous imperial enterprises and colonial exigencies.

Gilbert and Tompkins's contribution to post-colonial theatre is an extensive and rigorous theoretical examination and debate centred on the various projects of post-colonial theatre practitioners, performance, and modes of production. They offer invaluable re-examinations of canonical texts such as *The Tempest*, as reconsidered or 're-cited' by theatre practitioners of former colonial regions, as well as reassessing traditional, ritual, and carnival performance, the politics of language and translation, theory and politics of the post-colonial body, global neo-imperialism, and tourism.

The breadth and depth of theoretical analyses results in a complex and fascinating inter-disciplinary understanding of theatre praxis. Like Crow and Banfield, the authors are careful to situate political and historical contexts for the dramatic texts, performances, and forms that they discuss. However, they also offer the reader deconstructivist analyses which result in challenging and dynamic assessments of the ways in which post-colonial theatre practices have emerged and developed.

Perhaps the most crucial feature of this text is that it leaves the reader with an invigorating sense of the complexity of reading performance structures – from the text to the body – in theatre praxis that is not harnessed to western theatre traditions, thereby addressing in some detail debates ranging from spectatorship to the politics of language and translation.

This is an invaluable text for theatre/drama research and courses that are shaped by critical theories and inter-disciplinary approaches and perspectives. It refuses an understanding of post-coloniality by continents or countries alone and offers instead post-colonial performance as a field of political, cultural, social, and historical struggle not only between but within cultures. Such works – and here the extensive bibliography must be acknowledged – are vital for a continuing understanding of the involved and complex nature of theatre production and performance the world over.

NIKE IMORU

Linda Ben Zvi, ed.
Theater in Israel
University of Michigan Press, 1996.
ISBN 0-472-1067-4.

This book provides a useful introduction to theatre in Israel. The editor has commissioned and compiled essays by Israeli scholars and critics, written from the insiders' cultural and political points of view. Only a few Hebrew plays which have been translated and performed abroad have, up to now, received international attention. This book sets out to correct this situation by providing a firm historical background and surveying the major dramatic and theatrical achievements. The volume also contains dramatic and thematic analyses, interviews with playwrights, directors, and actors, a report on a symposium on Palestinian theatre, tables, and a bibliography, glossary, and index. The works of contemporary playwrights Yehoshua Sobol, Nissim Aloni, and Hanoch Levin are singled out for special analysis.

HANNA SCOLNICOV

William Tydeman and Steven Price
Wilde: Salomé
Cambridge: Cambridge University Press, 1996.
£11.95.
ISBN 0-521 -56545-6.

This latest volume admirably fulfils the premise of the 'Plays in Production' series: it shows how performance can both reflect and enlarge processes of historical change. The process is particularly noteworthy in the case of *Salomé* since the text has not always been respected by literary critics. Directors have seen what they missed,

recognizing a work that powerfully transgresses official boundaries. Tydeman and Price (and behind them Foucault) put this down to Wilde's own prophetic involvement in changing ideas of sexuality.

Frustratingly, there is little new to discover about the world premiere in Paris in 1896, but the authors' apparently aggrieved response on hearing that the role of a boy page had been given to a woman should stop us from assuming that the deepest subversion of *Salomé* relies on gender confusion. Outrageous representations of erotic desire have usually been more to the point. Tydeman and Price do much better with the first English stagings, with Reinhardt in 1903, with Evreinov in 1908, and the Maly in 1917. The Russian productions were the result of a moment when political revolution and sexual radicalism coincided. Something close to their storming spirit survived through to Kemp (1977) and arguably even Berkoff (1989).

Operatic, film, and dance versions are considered in a separate chapter. The problems of staging the 'Dance of the Seven Veils' in a way neither pornographic nor anodyne, and an insistent feeling that Wilde himself is often present, masked by one or more of his characters – these have been recurring issues. I would have liked more on the first English Herod, that sinisterly Wildean actor Robert Farquharson, and a broader survey of the influence of Aubrey Beardsley on set design. And it was Arthur Symons and not 'J. Arthur Symons' (presumably a conflation with John Addington Symonds) who was author of *The Daughters of Herodias*. But everyone gets those two muddled, and Tydeman and Price are, for the most part, extremely accurate and very well organized.

JOHN STOKES

Michael R. Booth and Joel H. Kaplan, eds.
The Edwardian Theatre:
Essays on Performance and the Stage
Cambridge: Cambridge University Press, 1996.
£30.00
ISBN 0-521-45375-5.

The bulk of these essays were originally delivered as papers at the 1992 conference entitled 'The Edwardian Stage' held at Vancouver Island, Canada. All are characterized by empirical research of a very high order, and as such the volume as a whole is probably of most value to scholars who already have an interest in Edwardian theatre and culture. Nevertheless, undergraduate and postgraduate students can usefully be directed to individual essays – especially the keynote essay, simply and aptly titled, 'What is the Edwardian Theatre?' The eclecticism of this essay is reflected in the range of those that follow, which most valuably extend our understanding of varied aspects of many different sorts of Edwardian theatrical activity and performance.

That said, a number of the essays reflect a growing interest in gender issues in this area: thus, there are essays on 'the girl' in musical comedy; on gender play and role reversal in the music hall; on the disadvantage women experienced in theatrical management; on suffragist theatre critics; and on Rebecca West's theatre criticism. There is also a revaluation of the dominant view of variety theatre during the Edwardian period, while other essays examine the audience for the 'New Drama', the development of Edwardian dramatic criticism, East End theatres, and stage and film versions of *The Whip*. This is an excellent volume whose contents, methodologies, and questioning of conventional definitions mark a major and very welcome contribution to scholarship on the Edwardian stage.

IAN CLARKE

Performance, Theory, General Studies

Michael Huxley and Noel Witts, eds.
Twentieth-Century Performance Reader
London; New York: Routledge, 1996. Pbk, £14.99.
ISBN 0-415-11628-7.

This book describes itself as 'pioneering', but such 'readers', with their role of bringing together materials from both distant and familiar archives, rarely are. The field of performance studies has been clearly suggested by, for example, Richard Schechner for many years. His NYU Performance Studies course takes museums as sites of performance and analyzes sex shows in its stride. Such frontiers make Witts's and Huxley's selection appear tame.

In the British context the book works well as a comprehensive and excellently laid out student guide with a useful cross-referencing system. But is there sense in publishing it so soon after Richard Drain's *Twentieth-Century Theatre: a Sourcebook* (1995), from the same publisher, which contains similar material from several of the same writers? Clearly it is tempting to lament omissions (Decroux is one that immediately springs to mind), yet the book succeeds in thought-provokingly placing key innovators of dance alongside theatre artists, composers, performance artists, and playwrights.

As such it will save teachers much time and effort, relieving them from library searches and photocopying. Yet what is the effect on students of 'readers' such as this ? Do they make students lazy, encourage surface reading rather than any

deeper acquaintance with theories and practitioners, or discourage exploratory use of the library? I hope that such works can be used as stimuli, but fear that in these times of immense pressure on students and staff alike they pander to the rhythm of the soundbite age.

In a few years the information gathered here will probably be available on-line to students for free at the click of a mouse. This makes all the more imperative the need for in-depth, individual, specialized studies of current practice rather than publishers' sops to the generalist or the familiar new breed of student – the name-dropper.

PAUL ALLAIN

Yvonne Daniel
**Rumba: Dance and Social Change
in Contemporary Cuba**
Bloomington: Indiana University Press, 1995.
ISBN 0-254-20948-X.

Rumba is a lively and stimulating investigation of Cuba's national dance in its cultural context, concentrating on Cuba's historical heritage and the effect of the mutitudinous influences in the dance. It also examines the dance in contemporary society, particularly the period from 1985 to 1990. Daniel gives an excellent analysis of the choreographic structure of the rumba, including verbal descriptions of the movement, music, dynamics, and form, as well as presenting notated music examples and actual dance steps. How rare it is, and how refreshing, to see Labanotation utilized to give clarity to the movement descriptions.

Daniel has written a very readable book. In its drawing together of an examination of the dance form, its cultural context, and its relationship to contemporary Cuban society it will be of interest to dancers, performers, dance historians, and anthropologists alike.

CLARE LIDBURY

Peter B. Murray
**Shakespeare's Imagined Persons:
the Psychology of Role-Playing and Acting**
London: Macmillan, 1996.
ISBN 0-333-63448-9.

Perhaps the most welcome aspect of Murray's book is his bold attempt to bring an interdisciplinary approach that incorporates experimental research derived from psychological enquiry to an analysis of acting. However, this is pursued not through a consideration of actors in performance as such, but through a detailed study of the principal characters of three of Shakespeare's plays: *Hamlet*, *Henry IV Part 1*, and *As You Like It*. Central to Murray's analyses are the ideas of

B. F. Skinner (set out cogently in the second chapter), whose language of radical behaviourism arose out of animal experiments, giving us such terms as 'operant conditioning' and 'schedules of reinforcement'.

Drawing on an impressive range of reference from Plato to Montaigne, Murray argues for a reformulation of such individuals' works in 'proto-behaviourist' terms, further proposing that 'Shakespeare's texts bear the distinctive marks of a behaviourist way of thinking' and that a 'Skinnerian analysis will illuminate the characters'.

So, in attempting to demonstrate the psychological coherence of Hamlet, the prince's actions are subjected to a comprehensive behaviourist treatment, the success of which may be judged to rest somewhat on the extent of the reader's sympathies with a Skinnerian point of view. For example: 'Hatred of his uncle makes it very reinforcing for Hamlet to believe the ghost'; 'Killing Claudius could still be aversive to Hamlet'; 'Hamlet urges Gertrude to reform by habituating herself to sexual abstinence'. The analysis is skilfully handled, but in seeking to account for the complexities of (fictional) human behaviour the application of technical language can seem reductive rather than illuminating.

Psychological research has shifted away from behaviourism to cognitive approaches in the last thirty years or so, unquestionably given impetus by Chomsky's convincing rout of Skinner's associative account of language learning. 'Unobservable' phenomena such as thoughts, feelings, emotions, and motivations fit uneasily within the behaviourist model. As it is precisely the relationship between these phenomena which are of interest to Murray in dissecting his characters' actions, it becomes necessary for him to speculate (while proposing 'chains' of behaviour) that 'a thought can respond to a thought, perhaps also reinforce it, and act as a stimulus for a further thought or action'.

However convincingly Skinnerian this may sound, the only possible verification for such an assertion is, unfortunately, the behaviourist's enemy – introspection. Another of Murray's acknowledged difficulties lies in the analytical limitation posed by Skinner's definition of the 'self' as 'a functionally unified system of responses'. Helpfully turning instead to Erving Goffman's dramaturgical model of role-playing and role-taking, explored most fully in the third (and, in my view, most interesting) chapter of the book, Murray's subsequent consideration of *As You Like It* seems more interesting for its absence of technical behaviourist language.

In the following, concluding chapter on 'Absorbed Action' (its focus Perdita's role-playing in *The Winter's Tale*), a more fully developed overview of the book as a whole would have been welcome. This is certainly not to say that Skinner's ideas may not be of considerable importance to the psychology of acting. As Murray points out, Stanislavsky's move towards the method of physical actions and away from the introspective broodings of actor 'as' character strike me as profoundly significant for actor training, consistent with the behaviourist notion that action comes first and post-hoc rationalizations of it afterwards. Murray has in fact taken a psychologically eclectic not a narrowly behaviourist focus in writing his book. He deserves congratulation for the wealth of fascinating material uncovered, which should prove a goldmine for future – including more explicitly performance-oriented – study.

CHRIS BANFIELD

David Johnston, ed.
Stages of Translation
Bath: Absolute Classics, 1996. £17.95.
ISBN 0-748-23075-4.

Absolute Classics has a good record for publishing new, actable versions of foreign plays. This volume gathers together essays by and interviews with twenty-six of its translators or adaptors, capably edited by David Johnston, whose interest in the Spanish theatre declares itself in the general composition of the book. Contributions range from the inane (Laurence Boswell's suggestion that a bad translation does not 'bamboozle' the reader by its language and thus gives instant access to 'the deeper meanings, the deeper themes' of the play) to the shrewdly sensible. The latter are generally from translators like Anthony Vivis and Eivor Martinus, with a proper knowledge of both source and target languages.

Many of the other contributors work either from literal versions supplied by someone else or venture dangerously upon their project with little Latin, French, Italian, Swedish, or whatever, and usually no Greek. Thus, many achieve what should always be acknowledged as 'versions' rather than translations, and it is disappointing to observe an emerging consensus that a memorable night in the theatre is associated more with the former than the latter. Cannot translators 'play feudal servant to their master' (Johnston) and produce texts that perform well? All in all, however, this is a sometimes intelligent and frequently thought-provoking contribution to the problems of translating for the theatre. It should be required reading for everyone who works in the field, either as translator or director.

MICHAEL ROBINSON